THE NEW MERMAIDS

The Shoemakers' Holiday

THE NEW MERMAIDS

General Editors

BRIAN MORRIS
Principal, St Davids University College, Lampeter

BRIAN GIBBONS
Professor of English, University of Leeds

The Shoemakers' Holiday

THOMAS DEKKER

Edited by

D. J. PALMER

*Professor of English Literature,
University of Manchester*

LONDON/ERNEST BENN LIMITED

NEW YORK/W. W. NORTON AND COMPANY INC.

First published in this form 1975
by Ernest Benn Limited
25 New Street Square, Fleet Street, London EC4A 3JA
Second impression 1981

© *Ernest Benn Limited 1975*

Published in the United States of America by
W. W. Norton and Company Inc.
500 Fifth Avenue, New York, N.Y. 10036

Distributed in Canada by
The General Publishing Company Limited · Toronto

Printed in Great Britain
by Fletcher & Son Ltd, Norwich

British Library Cataloguing in Publication Data

Dekker, Thomas
    The shoemaker's holiday.—(The new mermaids)
    I. Title   II. Palmer, D. J.
    III. Series
    822'.3   PR2490   80–42283

ISBN 0–510–33721–X
ISBN 0–393–90005–3 (U.S.A.)

CONTENTS

ACKNOWLEDGEMENTS

The following texts and works of reference have been consulted:

Bowers, F., ed., *The Dramatic Works of Thomas Dekker*, Vol. I, Cambridge, 1953.

Davies, P. C., ed., *The Shoemakers' Holiday*, Edinburgh, 1968.

Jones-Davies, M. T., *Un Peintre de la Vie Londonienne: Thomas Dekker*, 2 vols., Paris, 1958.

Mann, F. O., ed., *The Works of Thomas Deloney*, Oxford, 1912.

Pendry, E. D., ed., *Thomas Dekker*, The Stratford-upon-Avon Library 4, London, 1967.

Stow, J., *Survey of London* (1603 edn.), Everyman's Library, London, 1912.

The title-page of Q1 (1600) is reproduced from the Scolar Press facsimile of the British Museum copy (shelf-mark 161.b.1) by kind permission of the Scolar Press, Ltd., and of the Trustees of the British Museum. Norden's map of London is reproduced from the 1723 edition of *Speculum Britanniae* by kind permission of the Greater London Council Library.

INTRODUCTION

THE AUTHOR

THOMAS DEKKER was a Londoner all his life, but we cannot say with certainty when that life began or ended. In a pamphlet printed in 1632, he tells us that he is sixty years old, evidence which if accepted at its face value would mean that he was born in 1572. The same pamphlet may have been his last production, for one 'Thomas Decker, householder' was buried in Clerkenwell on 25 August 1632. We know nothing of his family background, but it is possible that he was of Dutch extraction; his name suggests so, and several of his works reflect an acquaintance with German literature.

Dekker seems to have begun his career as one of Philip Henslowe's stable of playwrights, working mainly in collaboration to provide the Admiral's Men with their repertoire. It is a measure of the insatiable demand of the Elizabethan public theatres for new material that in 1598 and 1599 alone Dekker had a hand in the preparation of at least twenty-five plays. In September 1598 Francis Meres included his name in *Palladis Tamia*, a tribute to contemporary writers, placing him among 'our best for Tragedie', though none of the plays that Meres had in mind have survived. The authorship of *The Shoemakers' Holiday* and *Old Fortunatus* is Dekker's alone; both plays were performed at Court during the Christmas festivities of 1599, and they were the first of his plays to be printed, in 1600. In the following year Dekker took sides with the Lord Chamberlain's Men, the company to which Shakespeare belonged, in the current 'War of the Theatres' by writing an attack on Ben Jonson in *Satiromastix*. This play was printed in 1602, but not before Jonson had retorted by pillorying Dekker in *The Poetaster*. In 1603 Dekker's career began to branch out in two other directions. He was commissioned, together with his recent adversary Jonson, to compose *The Magnificent Entertainment*, by which the city authorities intended to welcome the processional entry of the new monarch, King James. This was the first of several civic pageants that Dekker worked on, most of them belonging to his later years. The first of his pamphlets of London life, *The Wonderful Year*, also appeared in 1603.

Dekker's abiding interests were in the citizen life of his native London, in its domestic pieties and civic and patriotic virtues, as well as in the hardships and evils that were part of the contemporary scene. These are the charactertistic concerns of his dramatic work, which also reflects the fact that collaborative authorship was the rule rather than the exception in the professional theatre of his day. *Patient Grissil*, for instance, which takes up the domestic theme of the virtuous wife, was written with Henry Chettle and William Haughton, and printed in 1603. Thomas Middleton was his co-author in Part One of *The Honest Whore* (1604), a comedy with an Italian setting, but which deals with the conflicting social values of the gentry and the merchant class. Dekker was the sole author of *The Whore of Babylon* (1607), an allegorical celebration of Elizabeth's reign, but he joined forces with John Webster in two satirical citizen comedies, *Westward Ho!* and *Northward Ho!*, both printed in 1607. Working with Middleton again, he produced *The Roaring Girl* (1611), a comedy based on the romanticized adventures of Mary Frith, a notorious figure in contemporary London life. Dekker's later plays include two tragedies: *The Virgin Martyr* (1622), written with Philip Massinger after the manner of Beaumont and Fletcher, and *The Witch of Edmonton* (not printed until 1658), in collaboration with John Ford and William Rowley. By the end of his career, Dekker had been part-author of more than sixty plays, of which only seventeen have survived.

In the sequence of pamphlets that began in 1603 with *The Wonderful Year*, Dekker shows the same enjoyment of the vitality of citizen life, and the same compassion for poverty and distress, that are to be found in his plays. Such works as *News from Hell* (1606), *The Seven Deadly Sins of London* (1606), *The Bellman of London* (1608), *Lanthorn and Candlelight* (1608), and *The Gull's Hornbook* (1609) are not merely vivid descriptions of contemporary London. His gifts as a reporter of the daily scene rest upon a deep sense of communal values, intensified by the dangers of natural calamities such as the visitations of the plague and by the harsh inhumanity of economic exploitation.

Dekker's sympathy for the underprivileged and dispossessed, and the value he set upon patience in adversity, may well have been bred of personal experience. For despite his prolific output as a professional writer he seems to have been dogged throughout his career by financial insecurity. In 1598, near the beginning of his career, he was obliged to borrow money from Henslowe to obtain his release from a debtors' prison, and he was in prison for debt again from 1612 until 1619. If he was the Thomas Decker who died in Clerkenwell in 1632, it seems likely that he also died in debt, for his widow renounced her right to administer his estate.

DATE AND SOURCES

The date of *The Shoemakers' Holiday* is established by an entry in Henslowe's Diary for 15 July 1599, recording a payment of three pounds (probably the final instalment) for 'A Boocke of thomas dickers Called the gentle Craft'.

Dekker found the material for his play in Thomas Deloney's *The Gentle Craft*, a collection of stories which, as its title implies, celebrates the nobility of the shoemakers' trade. Such a title, almost certainly referring to Deloney's work, was entered in the Stationers' Register on 19 October 1597, and the collection presumably appeared in two parts shortly afterwards, although no copies of this original edition have survived. Dekker drew upon the three stories that comprise the first part, 'shewing what famous men have been Shoomakers in this Land, with their worthy deeds and great hospitality'. The first two of these tales concern princes who became shoemakers and saints, beginning with the legend of St Hugh. Hugh's love for Winifred is not returned, since she has devoted herself to God; after travelling abroad he takes up the trade of shoemaking, and finally meets a martyr's death with Winifred, his bones subsequently being made into shoemakers' tools. There follows the story of the royal brothers Crispine and Crispianus, who disguise themselves as shoemakers to escape the tyranny of the Emperor Maximinus. Eventually Crispine secretly marries the Emperor's daughter Ursula, while Crispianus wins glory in fighting for the French against the Persians, whose general Iphicratis is himself the son of a shoemaker and the legendary origin of the proverb, 'A shoemaker's son is a prince born'. In Dekker's play, this saying is turned into Simon Eyre's catch-phrase, 'Prince am I none, yet am I princely born', and the motifs of disguised nobility, constancy in love, travels abroad, and foreign war are woven into the sub-plots of the play.

For the central action of Eyre's rise to fame and fortune, Dekker was indebted to the third of Deloney's tales, which continues the theme of the proof of true nobility but inverts it by presenting a shoemaker who becomes a Lord Mayor, instead of a lord who becomes a shoemaker. Dekker's characterization of Eyre himself owes little to his shrewd but sober prototype in the source, yet the comic exuberance, liberality, and festive humour that Dekker embodies in Eyre are qualities that Deloney ascribes to the shoemakers as a class. 'The merry Shoomakers delight in good sport', writes Deloney, who also stresses the good fellowship, tolerance, and generosity that prevail among them: 'kind are they one to another, using each stranger as his brother'. Dekker imparts these virtues to his central character, and the mutual loyalty and high spirits that exist in Eyre's workshop express a sense of community that is contrasted with the false social values of the Lord Mayor (Sir Roger Otley), the Earl of Lincoln, and Hammon.

So Dekker remains true to Deloney's main theme, which is that in social merit and moral worth the shoemakers are not inferior to those of higher rank. He does, however, reshape and foreshorten Deloney's narrative material for dramatic purposes. In Deloney's account of Eyre's career, for instance, the central episode concerns the shoemaker's success, with the help of a foreign journeyman from his workshop, in passing himself off as an alderman in order to buy a valuable cargo on credit. By abbreviating this incident, Dekker considerably reduces, if he does not altogether eradicate, the element of fraudulent conspiracy involved in the transaction. The role of go-between, which is performed in the source by a Frenchman, is given in the play to Lacy in his disguise as Hans the Dutchman. A character of that name also figures in Deloney's story, which contains a sub-plot telling of the rivalry between three of Eyre's shoemakers, the Frenchman, the Dutchman, and Nicholas the Englishman, for the favours of Florence, the maid. Needless to say, Nicholas outwits both of his alien competitors and finally succeeds in marrying the girl. Dekker converts elements of the love-intrigue into the tricks by which Otley and Lincoln are deceived about the elopement of Lacy and Rose, and into the prevention of Hammon's marriage to Jane.

Dekker also extended the praise of the shoemakers' virtues by introducing a strong patriotic note, replacing romantic legend with national history. Whereas Deloney's Crispianus fought for the French against the Persians, Dekker's humble shoemaker Ralph fights for England against the French. The King who appears at the end of the play to take part in Eyre's Shrove Tuesday feast for the London apprentices has no counterpart in the source: Dekker makes him serve not only as an instrument of reconciliation and forgiveness, but as the personification of an ideal of national unity which Eyre and his shoemakers represent in microcosm. It seems that Dekker checked Deloney's account of Simon Eyre against the chronicles: from John Stow's *Survey of London* (1598), for instance, he could have discovered that the Lord Mayor at the time of Eyre's appointment as Sheriff was Sir Roger Otley, a name that does not occur in Deloney's tale. He would also have found in Stow that Simon Eyre was not a shoemaker at all, but an upholsterer and draper. Stow, like Deloney, somewhat ambiguously credits Eyre with building the Leadenhall, though in fact it was the name of an estate belonging to the city, upon which the historical Eyre erected a public granary in 1419, before his rise to civic office. The unnamed King of the play, who mingles so freely with his subjects, and who stands for a great national victory against the French, ought clearly to suggest Henry V, although historically Eyre's appointment as Sheriff in 1434 and as Lord Mayor in 1445 took place in the very different circumstances of the reign of Henry VI. Dekker therefore manipulated the historical background to suit his own dramatic purposes, perhaps because the Battle of Agincourt was fought on the Feast of St Crispian, a shoemakers' holiday that was currently being celebrated by a rival company in the newly-opened Globe playhouse.

THE PLAY

'Nothing is purposed but mirth', says the Epistle prefacing the printed play, an advertisement possibly intended to do double service, as an inducement to the purchaser, and as an assurance to the authorities that there is nothing in the play that will give them offence. The Epistle's description is a fair one, for *The Shoemakers' Holiday* is a genial and light-hearted comedy, a well-made entertainment seeking neither to instruct nor to reform us. That, of course, is not how the literary theorists of the age conceived comedy; they required considerably more than 'mirth'. But Dekker was writing for the popular stage, and while his play is in keeping with the general view of Renaissance criticism that comedy should deal with common life, and its domestic and civic concerns, in plain and colloquial diction, the carefree and indulgent spirit of *The Shoemakers' Holiday* hardly conforms with the learned emphasis on comedy's satirical function, an emphasis restated, for instance, by Sir Philip Sidney's definition of comedy in *An Apology for Poetry* (1595) as 'an imitation of the common errors of our life, which he representeth in the most ridiculous and scornful sort that may be, so as it is impossible that any beholder can be content to be such a one'. This learned idea of comedy, with the weight of critical authority behind it, was precisely what Ben Jonson brought to the popular stage in *Every Man Out of His Humour* during the same year that Dekker's play appeared.

If *The Shoemakers' Holiday* has few literary or intellectual pretensions by the standards of its time, to dismiss it as 'mere' entertainment would unjustly imply that it is frivolous and superficial. In fact, its 'mirth' belongs to a comic tradition that has its own conventions, even if they do not aspire to the dignity of a critical theory. Paradoxically, although the satirical conception of comedy was based upon classical models, the spirit of Dekker's play is paralleled in one of the earliest English imitations of Plautus, Nicholas Udall's *Ralph Roister Doister* (*c.* 1552), whose Prologue begins with this justification of 'mirth':

> What Creature is in health, eyther yong or olde,
> But som mirth with modestie wil be glad to use
> As we in thys Enterlude shall now unfolde,
> Wherin all scurilitie we utterly refuse,
> Avoiding such mirth wherin is abuse:
> Knowing nothing more comendable for a mans recreation
> Than Mirth which is used in an honest fashion:
> For Myrth prolongeth lyfe, and causeth health.
> Mirth recreates our spirites and voydeth pensivenesse,
> Mirth increaseth amitie, not hindring our wealth,
> Mirth is to be used both of more and lesse,
> Being mixed with vertue in decent comlynesse.

'Mirth', therefore, has therapeutic properties and a social function, counterparts to the corrective aims of satirical comedy. 'Mirth lengtheneth long life', as the prefatory Epistle affirms, to be corroborated by Simon Eyre in the play itself (e.g., III, iii, 22 and V. v, 20); it also promotes the harmony and wellbeing of the community. This identification of comedy with merry-making and conviviality, rather than with ridicule, signifies 'man's recreation' in the sense of pastime and in the deeper, etymological sense of the renewal of vital energies.

As the title of Dekker's play suggests, this spirit of comic 'mirth' is closely associated with popular traditions of holiday celebration. Whatever the remote origins of both comedy and tragedy in rituals enacted on sacred occasions (holy days), Dekker's festive shoemakers are kin to the medieval craft guilds that performed the mystery plays on the Feast of Corpus Christi. Those plays were a kind of holiday 'game' (so they are repeatedly called in the texts themselves), involving the whole community and, in their well-developed comic elements, giving a high-spirited but inoffensive outlet to the subversive and irreverent side of human nature. Festive revelry is a licence for the temporary release of natural energies and appetites from authority's constraint. So Dekker's comedy does not merely end in holiday: its entire action is informed by the values of licence and liberation. In their songs and dances, their drinking and feasting, their bawdy, anti-authoritarian jesting, and their stout-hearted comradeship, the shoemakers generate the exuberant spirit of festive comedy. Dekker took his cue from Deloney's praise of the hospitality, good fellowship, and sportive humour of 'the Gentle Craft', although there is no historical warrant for making Simon Eyre the founder of the apprentices' Shrove Tuesday feast, nor was that holiday the prerogative of the shoemakers. In fact, Shrove Tuesday in sixteenth-century London was notorious for the boisterous and often violent rampaging of the city's apprentices: Dekker converts such anarchic vitality to serve the purposes of comic justice and civic unity, creating in Simon Eyre a role similar to that of a Lord of Misrule, a traditional figure elected on certain holiday occasions to preside over the revels. The merry-making shoemakers are set in the framework of a plot which also involves release from various forms of restraint: while Eyre flouts at social distinctions in his 'madcap' progress from shoemaker to Lord Mayor, Lacy and Rose defy parental authority and the class barrier, and, at the point where the shoemakers' ebullient disregard for the restrictions of rank and order almost turns into a public riot, Jane is forcibly liberated from Hammon to be reunited with Ralph.

Complementary to the festive values of licence and liberation is the virtue of liberality, whose primary importance to the play makes it the theme of the opening lines:

> My Lord Mayor, you have sundry times
> Feasted myself and many courtiers more;
> Seldom or never can we be so kind
> To make requital of your courtesy.

Dekker introduces the theme ironically, for, as these lines reveal, Lincoln and Otley are a pair of prize snobs, the merchant's social ambition being matched by the nobleman's haughty condescension. Vanity and jealousy between the host and his guest are socially divisive, whereas true liberality is the agent of reciprocal goodwill and fellowship. Feasting is one of the main touchstones of liberality in the play, and Otley's narrow concern with using hospitality to gain social advantage is seen when he invites Hammon to 'a hunter's feast' (II. ii, 55), hoping 'To match my daughter to this gentleman', and when he courts the newly-affluent Eyre by entertaining him at Old Ford (III. iii). While Otley plays the host from motives of social prestige, the liberality of Lacy and Eyre promotes the festive spirit. In his disguise as Hans, Lacy celebrates his welcome into the fraternity of Eyre's workshop by ordering a round of drinks ('tap eens freelicke', I. iv, 108), while Eyre restores harmony in his household by similar means in II. iii. As Otley's guest at Old Ford (III. iii), Eyre soon takes charge of the proceedings, setting a tone of expansive mirth that draws unwonted laughter from his host; he then attempts to reconcile Otley and his daughter, and later he introduces the shoemakers to perform their morris dance. Eyre supplants Otley as the effective host at this feast just as he later succeeds him as Lord Mayor, and the junketing at Old Ford anticipates the great banquet generously presented by Eyre at the end of the play, when the fraternal conviviality of the shoe-makers spreads to the city and the nation as a whole.

The use of money is another touchstone of liberality in the play, also introduced early in the opening scene, through Lincoln's account of his nephew's prodigality: 'A verier unthrift lives not in the world'. Lincoln knows, of course, that to represent Lacy as a spendthrift will deter any ambitions that Otley may cherish to secure him as a son-in-law, but Lacy's extravagance reflects a generosity of spirit that his uncle and Rose's father lack. Moreover, Lacy's youthful prodigality has led him, his means being wasted, to learn the shoemaker's trade and become a useful member of society. Later in the opening scene Otley and Lincoln offer money to Lacy in an attempt to buy off his courtship of Rose and send him to the French wars, and subsequently (IV. v) they try unsuccessfully to bribe Firk into betraying the lovers' plot, while in V. ii Hammon insultingly offers Ralph twenty pounds for Jane. These attempts to make a commercial transaction out of the bonds of love and loyalty are contrasted with the liberality of Lacy and Eyre. The twenty 'portuguese' which the disguised Lacy lends to Eyre for a down-payment on the Dutch skipper's cargo (II. iii) is ironically the same money that he kept from his uncle's donation in the opening scene, after giving the rest to Askew (I. i, 107). The transaction which makes Eyre's fortune has an element of fraud in it, yet Dekker manages to suggest that Eyre is actually doing the Dutch skipper a favour by taking the cargo off his hands. Mutual profit, rather than mutual exploitation, is the benevolent notion of private enterprise that Eyre promotes, and it is appropriate that his civic munificence at the end of the play should include the building of the market at Leadenhall.

Fraud, perhaps, is too harsh a term to describe Eyre's dealings with the skipper, for trickery and deception belong to the spirit of comic licence in the play. There is a latent pun on 'the Gentle Craft' which occasionally becomes explicit, as, for instance, in Firk's jubilant self-congratulation after his gulling of Lincoln and Otley: 'Here's no craft in the Gentle Craft' (IV, v, 145). Ironically, while Lincoln and Otley suspect each other of 'subtlety' (e.g., I. i, 38 and 71), they suspect nobody else. Lacy is the play's most skilful dissimulator, and the parallels between his disguise to gain Rose and Eyre's masquerade as an alderman to make his fortune suggest how each is to be regarded.

Lacy's decision 'To clothe his cunning with the Gentle Craft' (I. iii, 4) is likely to provoke a mixed response in the audience. He is, after all, an army deserter in time of war, a point which the play emphasizes by contrasting him with Ralph, who is unable to obtain exemption from military service although he has equally compassionate grounds. Lacy dishonours his birth and his duty, yet his disguise also provides the means of redeeming himself by the honest industry of shoemaking, and, more importantly, by help-ing Eyre to his fortune. While Lacy discards the trappings of high rank, Eyre assumes them, and his rise to civic status begins with another equivocal use of disguise. We are not told why the Dutch merchant 'dares not show his head' (II. iii, 17), a circumstance which is not in Deloney's tale, but the implication must be that he cannot sell his cargo openly because he is on the wrong side of the law, perhaps for evading duties. When Eyre dresses as an alderman, therefore, and promises the skipper 'thou shalt have my countenance in the city' (II. iii, 138), he is deceiving the skipper, conniving at the skipper's offence, and compounding the felony by impersonating a civic officer. If this rather shady deal is to be condoned, it is partly because comic licence prefers a good piece of trickery to the strict observance of law, and partly because Dekker works within a convention that treats disguise as a liberation, rather than a con-cealment, of the true self. In becoming the shoemaker Hans, Lacy proves himself to be more lively and versatile than the colourless stereotype of the romantic lover: he entertains his workmates, shares their sense of fun, and takes the opportunity of handsomely requiting Eyre's kindness to him. Similarly, when Eyre poses as an alderman, he comes out in his true colours, both as the shrewd trickster we have previously glimpsed in II. iii (when he resolved a minor industrial dispute by calling aloud for twelve cans of beer but privately reducing the order to two), and as the head and spokesman of his community. 'Why, now you look like yourself, master', (II. iii, 112) says Hodge when Eyre puts on his borrowed robes. By playing the alderman, Eyre eventually becomes Lord Mayor, but he not only remains himself in the process, he finds increasing scope to display that self.

Interwoven with the fortunes of Lacy and Rose and the progress of Eyre are the vicissitudes of Ralph and Jane, who do not provide much in the way of comic 'mirth'. Yet if the pathos that informs their story counterbalances the hearty humour prevailing in the rest of the play, their constancy in misfortune is another aspect of the play's concern with loyalty. We are not allowed to regard either of them sentimentally: Firk and Margery prevent that with their somewhat unfeeling jests at the expense of the couple's predicaments, at their parting in the opening scene, at the return of Ralph in III. ii, and at Ralph's discovery that his wife is about to marry Hammon in IV. iii. The parallels between this pair and Lacy and

Rose are neatly drawn: Hammon pays unsuccessful court to each
of the girls in turn, and in both cases a shoe reunites the lovers (as
in *Cinderella*), yet the romantic charm which invests the situation of
Lacy and Rose is strongly contrasted with the more realistic treat-
ment of Ralph and Jane. The return of Ralph from the wars, lame
and unheralded, awkwardly obtruding on a scene of excitement and
imminent rejoicing at Eyre's elevation to Sheriff (III. ii), is surely
the finest moment in the play, as a sudden and moving diversion of
our sympathies. Ralph's exchange with Hammon's servant (IV. iii)
is also very effectively managed, both in the clash of social attitudes
and in Ralph's stunned incredulity. Indeed, Ralph seems to have
engaged Dekker's creative interest more than any other character
except Eyre himself.

The language of the play is neither subtle nor complex, but if it
lacks richness or brilliance of texture, it is nevertheless lively and
efficient stage-dialogue, closely trimmed to the action and sufficiently
well-sprung to generate and sustain the dramatic tension of each
scene. The play contains a variety of styles, according to character,
social status, and romantic or comic function. Verse is spoken by the
'serious' characters, chiefly by those of higher rank, but also by
Ralph and Jane at moments charged with sentiment, while prose is
the medium of Simon Eyre and his household, including Lacy in his
disguise.

Dominant among the various styles is Eyre's vein of ebullient
cajolery and exhortation, which is the main vehicle of the play's
comic energies. Eyre's distinctive idiom serves both as an assertion
of his authority over an unruly household and as an expression of
his own irreverence. Instead of quelling the lively spirit of in-
subordination, his tirades shrewdly convert dissension into good-
natured raillery and merry-making, in which aggressive vitality
serves the cause of social harmony:

Away, you Islington whitepot! Hence, you hopperarse, you barley
pudding full of maggots, you broiled carbonado! Avaunt, avaunt,
Mephostophilus! Shall Sim Eyre learn to speak of you, Lady
Madgy? Vanish, Mother Miniver-cap, vanish, go, trip and go,
meddle with your partlets and your pishery-pashery, your flewes
and your whirligigs! Go, rub out of mine alley! Sim Eyre knows
how to speak to a Pope, to Sultan Soliman, to Tamburlaine, and
he were here: and shall I melt, shall I droop before my Sovereign?
No! Come, my Lady Madgy; follow me, Hans; about your business,

my frolic free-booters; Firk, frisk about and about and about, for
the honour of mad Sim Eyre, Lord Mayor of London. (V. iv, 49–60)

The vigour and inventiveness of Eyre's prose depends on a few
relatively simple rhetorical devices: parallelism, alliteration, the use
of catch-phrases, and the incongruous mingling of the homely with
the exotic, of the low register with the high, together create an
impression of rhythmic and racy speech, instinct with personality
and with the exuberant libertarian values that triumph in the play
as a whole. The dependence of this comic prose upon certain
recognizable mannerisms heightens rather than diminishes its
effectiveness. Despite its close reference to the everyday world in-
habited by its original audiences, it is essentially a style that belongs
to the stage rather than to the streets of Elizabethan London: in
fact, to judge from his allusions to 'Mephostophilus', 'Sultan Soliman', and 'Tamburlaine', Eyre is something of a playgoer himself.

Firk's addiction to the pun, usually with indecent intent, gives
a linguistic dimension to the play's concern with festive release, for
his incessant wordplay activates the latent unruly energies of
language. He is the clown of the play, and his verbal trickery, with
its double meanings and sly innuendoes, parallels the duplicities,
coincidences, and accidental recognitions that occur in the plot.
Words undergo displacement in his quibbles just as characters
change their social roles in the action of the play. However, Firk's
unsophisticated humour needs no dignifying: as the clown, he reduces
the unrestrained indulgence of natural appetite to its simplest and
most basic level in his bawdy jokes and his relish for 'good cheer',
whether it is ale or the more sumptuous delights promised by the
'pancake bell' (V. ii, 194). His name itself, particularly when he and
his master make a verb of it, suggests vigorous animal activity: it
becomes a kind of pun, frolicsome and obscene. Firk's perpetual
jesting has little regard for the feelings of others, friends or enemies.
Some of his quips seem tactless, if not heartless; for instance, at the
parting of Ralph and Jane in the opening scene, while he also shows
scant sympathy with Ralph's agitation at the discovery of Jane's
whereabouts in IV. iii. He finds Lacy's Dutch uproariously funny
in I. iv, and insists on treating the supposed foreigner as an amiable
buffoon, an attitude said to be not uncommon among Englishmen.
Firk embodies the clannish *élan* of the shoemakers at its most
assertive, and although his disrespect is not malicious, there is a

certain vindictiveness in his enjoyment of an advantage over social superiors, particularly in the encounters with Lincoln, Otley, and Hammon (IV. v and V. ii). His irrepressible and irresponsible nature is complemented by the sober and conscientious character of Hodge, and by Margery's ill-managed airs of ladylike refinement. The trio, in effect, seem conceived as projections of different aspects of Eyre himself: his love of merry-making, his shrewd business sense, and his aspiration to 'worshipful' status.

Lacy's stage-Dutch adds another dimension to the play's linguistic range. It solves the dramatic difficulty of introducing Lacy into the company of the comedians while preserving his status as a 'straight' character. By becoming a foreigner, Lacy adopts a speech that is neither in the courtly manner of his verse nor in the low style of his workmates' comic prose: it is a nonce-language which manages to sound sufficiently Dutch to English ears without becoming completely incomprehensible. Lacy has presumably learned his Dutch where he learned shoemaking, in Wittenberg (I. i, 29), for the distinction between Dutch and 'Deutsch' was not as specific in Dekker's time as it has become since the founding of the German state. Possibly Dekker's own ethnic origins account for the way in which he has developed Lacy's disguise from the English-speaking Dutchman of Deloney's tale, but the role of Hans is also related to the play's patriotic theme. Although Wittenberg is geographically remote from the Low Countries, to the Elizabethans both were identified with Protestant militancy: Wittenberg had its associations with Martin Luther, while the Low Countries were the theatre of war in which English armies were supporting the struggle of Dutch and Flemish Protestants against their Spanish overlords. In a play set against the background of war with the French, therefore, Lacy's guttural accents served not only to amuse but to stir the sympathies of an Elizabethan audience.

The verse of the play lacks the animation and invention of the comic prose; its rhythms are less assured and its texture somewhat thin. Nevertheless it is serviceable dramatic verse, propelling the action forward with clarity and economy. Dekker can also turn his poetic limitations to dramatic advantage, as in the wooing scenes that Hammon plays with Rose (II. ii and III. i) and then with Jane (IV. i), parallel scenes in which the stilted artifice of the stychomythia and outworn Petrarchan conceits reveals the ineptness of Hammon's pretensions as a lover. In each of his ill-judged *amours*, the luckless

Hammon eventually discards the mask of the courtly suitor to expose a brash, insensitive nature. He is an interesting study in false gentility, and his role resembles that of the conventional comic butt whose defeat and expulsion leads to the triumphant renewal and reintegration of society. Hammon's final discomfiture and withdrawal are treated with Dekker's characteristic tolerance, allowing him a measure of our sympathy, but he is excluded from the feasting and reconciliation in which even the mean-spirited Lincoln and Otley are permitted to participate.

The Shoemakers' Holiday is sometimes read as a picture of the exuberant life of Elizabethan London, or as a reflection of the social and economic attitudes of the rising middle class, but its documentary value is slight compared with its dramatic interest as a comedy. Indeed, precisely because it is a comedy, based on dramatic principles and conventions, it is likely to mislead the reader who treats it as realistic and reliable evidence of the social conditions of the period. The artistry of the play depends no more upon the historical authenticity of its comic world than it does upon intellectual complexity or brilliance of literary style, qualities it does not possess. Dekker's skill is rather to be seen in the shaping of his material into a compact well-proportioned design; character, situation, and dialogue are conceived in terms of the rhythms of stage-performance, and these are the terms in which the text of the play should be read. *The Shoemakers' Holiday* has been called 'an Elizabethan pantomime', a description not altogether inappropriate, although it carries the patronizing and unjust implication that its concerns are somehow not adult. Its concerns, in fact, are with no less a subject than the health and vitality of the corporate life of which we are all members, and of which the theatre itself is an embodiment.

NOTE ON THE TEXT

Although six editions of *The Shoemakers' Holiday* were published by 1657, the first Quarto (Q1) of 1600 has sole authority. The present edition is based on the Scolar Press facsimile of a British Museum copy of Q1 (Shelf-mark: 161.b.1), checked against the text of Fredson Bowers's old-spelling edition in *The Dramatic*

Works of Thomas Dekker, vol. I (Cambridge, 1953), and modernized in spelling and punctuation.

Q1 is a black-letter text, with some metrical irregularities and inconsistencies in the speech-headings; it probably derives, as Bowers argues, from 'carelessly and incompletely revised foul papers'. It does not mention an author, nor was it entered in the Stationers' Register, although the reference in Henslowe's Diary establishes Dekker's authorship, while the printer of Q1, Valentine Sims, had rights in his copy which he transferred to John Wright, the printer of Q2, in 1610. In Q1, the play is called *The Shoemakers' Holiday* on the title-page only; its running-title is 'A pleasant Comedie of . . . the Gentle Craft'.

Most of the emendations adopted or proposed in Bowers's conservative edition have been followed here, except at IV. ii, 12 and V. v, 151. There is no act or scene division in Q1; the present edition follows that of Bowers, except for the division between Acts III and IV. In this case, III. iii (the banquet scene at Old Ford) has been preferred as the final scene of Act III, since the following scene, between Jane and Hammon, initiates a new development in the plot. By concluding Act III with the third scene, moreover, a suitable point for an interval is provided by the climactic anticipation of the play's final feasting scene. Lacy's stage-Dutch has been reproduced in its original spelling.

ABBREVIATIONS

ed.	editor
N.E.D.	New English Dictionary
om.	omits
Q1	First Quarto of 1600
s.d.	stage direction
s.p.	speech prefix

FURTHER READING

Editions

Bowers, F., *The Dramatic Works of Thomas Dekker*. Vol. I, Cambridge, 1953.

Davies, P. C., *The Shoemakers' Holiday*. Edinburgh, 1968.

Steane, J. B., *The Shoemaker's Holiday*. Cambridge, 1965.

Books

Gregg, K. L., *Thomas Dekker: A Study in Economic and Social Backgrounds*. Seattle, 1924.

Hunt, M. L., *Thomas Dekker: A Study*. New York, 1911.

Jones-Davies, M. T., *Un Peintre de la Vie Londonienne: Thomas Dekker*. 2 vols. Paris, 1958.

Price, G. R., *Thomas Dekker*. New York, 1969.

Articles

Brown, A., 'Citizen Comedy and Domestic Drama', *Jacobean Theatre*. Ed. J. R. Brown and B. Harris. Stratford-upon-Avon Studies I. 1960.

Ferguson, W. C.. 'The Compositors of *2 Henry IV*, *Much Ado About Nothing*, *The Shoemakers' Holiday* and *The First Part of the Contention*', *Studies in Bibliography*, XIII, 1960.

George, J., 'Four Notes on the Text of Dekker's *The Shoemakers'*
Holiday', *Notes and Queries*, CXCIV, 1949.

Kaplan, J. H., 'Virtue's Holiday: Thomas Dekker and Simon Eyre',
Renaissance Drama, New Series II, 1969.

McNeir, W. F., 'The Source of Simon Eyre's Catch-Phrase',
Modern Language Notes, LIII, 1938.

Manheim, L. M., 'The King in Dekker's *The Shoemakers' Holiday*',
Notes and Queries, New Series IV, 1957.

Toliver, H. E., '*The Shoemakers' Holiday*: Theme and Image',
Boston University Studies in English, V, 1961.

Mercers

Grocers

Drapers

Fishmongers

Goldsmiths

Skinners

The new Burn...

Grays Inn

The Temple

Leiceser house

The Temple

White Friers

Bridewell

Black Friers

Black Friers

Paule Wharfe

Broken Wharfe

Quene hithe

T H A M E S

Banke side

Lambeth marsh

The Bear house

play house

play house

Norden's map of London (1

Speculum Britanniae

THE
SHOMAKERS
Holiday.
OR
The Gentle Craft.

With the humorous life of Simon
Eyre, ſhoomaker, and Lord Maior
of London.

As it was acted before the Queenes moſt excellent Ma-
ieſtie on New-yeares day at night laſt, by the right
honourable the Earle of Notingham, Lord high Ad-
mirall of England, his ſeruants.

Printed by Valentine Sims dwelling at the foote of Adling
hill, neere Bainards Caſtle, at the ſigne of the White
Swanne, and are there to be ſold.
1 6 0 0.

TO ALL GOOD FELLOWS, PROFESSORS OF THE GENTLE CRAFT, OF WHAT DEGREE SOEVER

Kind gentlemen and honest boon companions, I present you here with a merry conceited comedy, called *The Shoemakers' Holiday*, acted by my Lord Admiral's players this present Christmas before the Queen's most excellent Majesty; for the mirth and pleasant matter by her Highness graciously accepted, being indeed no way offensive. The argument of the play I will set down in this epistle: Sir Hugh Lacy, Earl of Lincoln, had a young gentleman of his own name, his near kinsman, that loved the Lord Mayor's daughter of London; to prevent and cross which love, the Earl caused his kinsman to be sent coronel of a company into France; who resigned his place to another gentleman, his friend, and came disguised like a Dutch shoemaker to the house of Simon Eyre in Tower Street, who served the Mayor and his household with shoes; the merriments that passed in Eyre's house, his coming to be Mayor of London, Lacy's getting his love, and other accidents, with two merry three-men's songs. Take all in good worth that is well intended, for nothing is purposed but mirth: mirth lengtheneth long life, which with all other blessings I heartily wish you.
                              Farewell.

2 *conceited* wittily devised
11 *coronel* colonel
17 *three-men's songs* songs for three voices

THE GENTLE CRAFT. See Introduction, p. ix
3 *my Lord Admiral's players.* The principal rivals of Shakespeare's company, the Lord Chamberlain's men. Edward Alleyn was their leading actor, their repertory included plays by Marlowe, and they performed at the Rose Theatre, owned by Philip Henslowe.

THE FIRST THREE-MAN'S SONG

O the month of May, the merry month of May,
So frolic, so gay, and so green, so green, so green;
O and then did I unto my true love say,
Sweet Peg, thou shalt be my Summer's Queen.

Now the Nightingale, the pretty Nightingale,   5
The sweetest singer in all the forest's choir,
Entreats thee, sweet Peggy, to hear thy true love's tale:
Lo, yonder she sitteth, her breast against a brier.

But O I spy the Cuckoo, the Cuckoo, the Cuckoo;
See where she sitteth, come away my joy: 10
Come away I prithee, I do not like the Cuckoo
Should sing where my Peggy and I kiss and toy.

O the month of May, the merry month of May,
So frolic, so gay, and so green, so green, so green;
And then did I unto my true love say,   15
Sweet Peg, thou shalt be my Summer's Queen.

THE FIRST THREE-MAN'S SONG. There is no indication where
this should be sung in the play, but an appropriate point would be in
III. iii, when the shoemakers perform their morris dance, and Rose
recognizes Lacy.
8 *her breast against a brier.* The sweet song of the nightingale was supposed
to be caused by the pain of a thorn in her side.
9 *the Cuckoo.* The name suggests cuckoldry: cf. *Love's Labour's Lost*,
V. ii, 897–8, 'Cuckoo, cuckoo—O word of fear, / Unpleasing to a married
ear'.

THE SECOND THREE-MAN'S SONG

This is to be sung at the latter end
Cold's the wind, and wet's the rain,
  Saint Hugh be our good speed;
Ill is the weather that bringeth no gain,
  Nor helps good hearts in need.

Trowl the bowl, the jolly nut-brown bowl,   5
  And here kind mate to thee;
Let's sing a dirge for Saint Hugh's soul,
  And down it merrily.

Down a down, hey down a down,
  Hey derry derry, down a down; *Close with the tenor boy* 10
Ho well done, to me let come,
  Ring compass gentle joy.

Trowl the bowl, the nut-brown bowl,
  And here kind &c. *as often as there be men to drink*

At last when all have drunk, this verse:
Cold's the wind, and wet's the rain,   15
  Saint Hugh be our good speed;
Ill is the weather that bringeth no gain,
  Nor helps good hearts in need.

---

5 *Trowl* pass round
12 *Ring compass* the full range of harmony, or possibly 'complete the circle'

---

at the latter end. Either to conclude the play, after the King's final speech,
or at the beginning of IV. ii, where the shoemakers are singing 'Hey
down a down, down derry'.
2 *Saint Hugh.* Patron saint of the shoemakers. See Introduction, p. ix.

THE PROLOGUE AS IT WAS PRONOUNCED
BEFORE THE QUEEN'S MAJESTY

As wretches in a storm, expecting day,
With trembling hands and eyes cast up to heaven,
Make prayers the anchor of their conquered hopes,
So we, dear Goddess, wonder of all eyes,
Your meanest vassals, through mistrust and fear   5
To sink into the bottom of disgrace
By our imperfit pastimes, prostrate thus
On bended knees, our sails of hope do strike,
Dreading the bitter storms of your dislike.
Since then, unhappy men, our hap is such   10
That to ourselves ourselves no help can bring,
But needs must perish, if your saint-like ears,
Locking the temple where all mercy sits,
Refuse the tribute of our begging tongues:
Oh grant, bright mirror of true chastity,   15
From those life-breathing stars your sun-like eyes,
One gracious smile: for your celestial breath
Must send us life, or sentence us to death.

[DRAMATIS PERSONAE

KING OF ENGLAND
EARL OF LINCOLN
EARL OF CORNWALL
SIR ROGER OTLEY, *Lord Mayor of London*
SIMON EYRE, *shoemaker and afterwards Lord Mayor*
ROWLAND LACY, *nephew to Lincoln, afterwards disguised as Hans Meulter*
ASKEW, *cousin to Lacy*
HAMMON, *a city gentleman*
WARNER, *cousin to Hammon*
MASTER SCOTT, *friend to Otley*
HODGE (*also called* ROGER), *foreman to Eyre*
FIRK, *journeyman to Eyre*
RALPH DAMPORT, *journeyman to Eyre*
LOVELL, *servant to the King*
DODGER, *parasite to Lincoln*
Dutch Skipper
Boy, *apprentice to Eyre*
Boy, *servant to Otley*
Servingman *to Hammon*
MARGERY, *wife to Eyre*
ROSE, *daughter to Otley*
JANE, *wife to Ralph Damport*
SYBIL, *maid to Rose*
Noblemen, Soldiers, Huntsmen, Shoemakers, Apprentices, Servants]

A PLEASANT COMEDY OF THE GENTLE CRAFT

[Act I, Scene i]

Enter LORD MAYOR [*and*] LINCOLN

LINCOLN

My Lord Mayor, you have sundry times
Feasted myself and many courtiers more;
Seldom or never can we be so kind
To make requital of your courtesy.
But leaving this, I hear my cousin Lacy   5
Is much affected to your daughter Rose.

LORD MAYOR

True, my good Lord, and she loves him so well
That I mislike her boldness in the chase.

LINCOLN

Why, my Lord Mayor, think you it then a shame
To join a Lacy with an Otley's name?   10

LORD MAYOR

Too mean is my poor girl for his high birth;
Poor citizens must not with courtiers wed,
Who will in silks and gay apparel spend
More in one year than I am worth by far.
Therefore your Honour need not doubt my girl.   15

1 *sundry* several
5 *cousin* kinsman
15 *doubt* fear, mistrust

A PLEASANT COMEDY OF THE GENTLE CRAFT. The
running title of the play in Q1: *The Shoemakers' Holiday* appears only
on the title page.
LORD MAYOR. So he is named in Q1 stage directions and speech prefixes
throughout, even after Eyre has become Lord Mayor; since confusion is
unlikely, this edition follows suit.

LINCOLN

  Take heed, my Lord, advise you what you do:
  A verier unthrift lives not in the world
  Than is my cousin, for, I'll tell you what,
  'Tis now almost a year since he requested
  To travel countries for experience;   20
  I furnished him with coin, bills of exchange,
  Letters of credit, men to wait on him,
  Solicited my friends in Italy
  Well to respect him, but see the end:
  Scant had he journeyed through half Germany,   25
  But all his coin was spent, his men cast off,
  His bills embezzled, and my jolly coz,
  Ashamed to show his bankrupt presence here,
  Became a shoemaker in Wittenberg:
  A goodly science for a gentleman   30
  Of such descent! Now judge the rest by this.
  Suppose your daughter have a thousand pound,
  He did consume me more in one half-year;
  And make him heir to all the wealth you have,
  One twelve-month's rioting will waste it all.   35
  Then seek, my Lord, some honest citizen
  To wed your daughter to.

LORD MAYOR   I thank your Lordship.
  [aside] Well, fox, I understand your subtlety.
  As for your nephew, let your Lordship's eyes
  But watch his actions, and you need not fear,   40
  For I have sent my daughter far enough;
  And yet your cousin Rowland might do well
  Now he hath learned an occupation.
  [aside] And yet I scorn to call him son-in-law.

LINCOLN

  Ay, but I have a better trade for him: 45
  I thank his Grace he hath appointed him
  Chief colonel of all those companies
  Mustered in London and the shires about

25 *Scant* scarcely
27 *embezzled* wasted
35 *rioting* riotous living, extravagance
41 *sent* ed. (om. Q1)

To serve his Highness in those wars of France.
See where he comes: Lovell, what news with you?   50
Enter LOVELL, LACY *and* ASKEW

LOVELL

My Lord of Lincoln, 'tis his Highness' will
That presently your cousin ship for France
With all his powers: he would not for a million
But they should land at Deepe within four days.

LINCOLN

Go certify his Grace it shall be done.   55

Exit LOVELL

Now, cousin Lacy, in what forwardness
Are all your companies?

LACY   All well prepared:
The men of Hertfordshire lie at Mile End,
Suffolk and Essex train in Tothill-fields,
The Londoners and those of Middlesex,   60
All gallantly prepared in Finsbury,
With frolic spirits long for their parting hour.

LORD MAYOR

They have their imprest, coats and furniture,
And if it please your cousin Lacy come
To the Guildhall, he shall receive his pay,   65
And twenty pounds beside my brethren
Will freely give him, to approve our loves
We bear unto my Lord your uncle here.

LACY

I thank your Honour.

LINCOLN   Thanks, my good Lord Mayor.

LORD MAYOR

At the Guildhall we will expect your coming.   70

Exit [LORD MAYOR]

52 *presently* immediately
53 *powers* forces
54 *Deepe* Dieppe
63 *imprest* recruitment pay
63 *furniture* equipment

58–61 *Mile End . . . Tothill-fields . . . Finsbury.* Three drilling grounds out-
    side the city walls, respectively to the east, west, and north. That in
    Finsbury was used for archery (cf. Firk's reference in II. iii, 60).

LINCOLN

To approve your loves to me? No, subtlety!
Nephew, that twenty pound he doth bestow
For joy to rid you from his daughter Rose.
But, cousins both, now here are none but friends,
I would not have you cast an amorous eye   75
Upon so mean a project as the love
Of a gay, wanton, painted citizen.
I know this churl, even in the height of scorn,
Doth hate the mixture of his blood with thine:
I pray thee do thou so. Remember, coz,   80
What honourable fortunes wait on thee:
Increase the King's love, which so brightly shines
And gilds thy hopes; I have no heir but thee—
And yet not thee, if with a wayward spirit
Thou start from the true bias of my love.   85

LACY

My Lord, I will for honour, not desire
Of land or livings, or to be your heir,
So guide my actions in pursuit of France
As shall add glory to the Lacys' name.

LINCOLN

Coz, for those words here's thirty portuguese,   90
And nephew Askew, there's a few for you.
Fair Honour in her loftiest eminence
Stays in France for you till you fetch her thence.
Then, nephews, clap swift wings on your designs:
Begone, begone, make haste to the Guildhall.   95
There presently I'll meet you; do not stay:
Where Honour beckons, shame attends delay.
                                         Exit [LINCOLN]

ASKEW

How gladly would your uncle have you gone!

---

97 *beckons* ed. (becomes Q1)

---

85 *true bias.* Proper course: an image from the game of bowls, in which the
   bowl is weighted to roll in a curve.
90 *portuguese.* A gold coin worth about 4 pounds: Lincoln makes a handsome gesture, but twenty of these portuguese are later lent by Lacy to
   Eyre as the down-payment on the Dutch skipper's cargo (II. iii, 24).

LACY

    True, coz, but I'll o'erreach his policies.
    I have some serious business for three days,   100
    Which nothing but my presence can dispatch.
    You therefore, cousin, with the companies
    Shall haste to Dover; there I'll meet with you,
    Or, if I stay past my prefixed time,
    Away for France: we'll meet in Normandy.   105
    The twenty pounds my Lord Mayor gives to me
    You shall receive, and these ten portuguese,
    Part of mine uncle's thirty. Gentle coz,
    Have care to our great charge: I know your wisdom
    Hath tried itself in higher consequence.   110

ASKEW

    Coz, all myself am yours; yet have this care,
    To lodge in London with all secrecy:
    Our uncle Lincoln hath, besides his own,
    Many a jealous eye that in your face
    Stares only to watch means for your disgrace.   115

LACY

    Stay, cousin: who be these?

Enter SIMON EYRE, MARGERY, HODGE, FIRK, JANE, *and* RALPH
with a piece

EYRE

    Leave whining, leave whining; away with this whimpering,
    this puling, these blubbering tears, and these wet eyes. I'll
    get thy husband discharged, I warrant thee, sweet Jane:
    go to!   120

HODGE

    Master, here be the captains.

EYRE

    Peace, Hodge; husht, ye knave, husht!

FIRK

    Here be the cavaliers and the coronels, master.

---

  99 *o'erreach his policies* outwit his scheming
109 *charge* commission
    s.d. *with a piece* a firing-piece, a gun
118 *puling* snivelling
123 *cavaliers and . . . coronels* officers, commanders

EYRE

Peace, Firk; peace, my fine Firk! Stand by with your
pishery-pashery, away! I am a man of the best presence: 125
I'll speak to them and they were Popes! Gentlemen, captains, colonels, commanders: brave men, brave leaders,
may it please you to give me audience? I am Simon Eyre,
the mad shoemaker of Tower Street; this wench with the
mealy mouth that will never tire is my wife, I can tell you;   130
here's Hodge, my man and my foreman; here's Firk, my
fine firking journeyman; and this is blubbered Jane. All we
come to be suitors for this honest Ralph: keep him at home,
and as I am a true shoemaker and a gentleman of the Gentle
Craft, buy spurs yourself, and I'll find ye boots these seven   135
years.

MARGERY

Seven years, husband?

EYRE

Peace, midriff, peace! I know what I do: peace!

FIRK

Truly, master cormorant, you shall do God good service to
let Ralph and his wife stay together. She's a young new-   140
married woman; if you take her husband away from her
a-night, you undo her; she may beg in the daytime, for he's
as good a workman at a prick and an awl as any is in our trade.

JANE

O let him stay, else I shall be undone!

FIRK

Ay, truly, she shall be laid at one side like a pair of old shoes   145
else, and be occupied for no use.

124 *Stand by* Out of the way
125 *pishery-pashery* fuss
125 *of the best presence* fit for the noblest company
130 *mealy mouth* genteel way of talking
132 *journeyman* one who has served his apprenticeship

---

132 *firking*. Frisking: Firk's name lends itself to a variety of meanings in
    different contexts throughout the play, all suggesting lively and
    vigorous activity, and many of them bawdy.
138 *midriff*. A reference to Margery's diminutive stature, or possibly to her
    sex as 'Adam's rib'.
139 *cormorant*. Firk's corruption of 'coronel'.
143-6 *prick and an awl ... undone ... occupied*. Bawdy quibbles.

LACY

Truly, my friends, it lies not in my power;
The Londoners are pressed, paid, and set forth
By the Lord Mayor: I cannot change a man.

HODGE

Why, then you were as good be a corporal as a colonel, if 150
you cannot discharge one good fellow; and I tell you true,
I think you do more than you can answer, to press a man
within a year and a day of his marriage.

EYRE

Well said, melancholy Hodge! Gramercy, my fine foreman!

MARGERY

Truly, gentlemen, it were ill done for such as you to stand 155
so stiffly against a poor young wife: considering her case,
she is new-married, but let that pass. I pray, deal not roughly
with her; her husband is a young man and but newly
entered, but let that pass.

EYRE

Away with your pishery-pashery, your polls and your 160
edipolls! Peace, midriff; silence, Cicely Bumtrinket! Let
your head speak.

FIRK

Yea, and the horns too, master.

EYRE

Tawsoone, my fine Firk, tawsoone! Peace, scoundrels!
See you this man, captains? You will not release him? Well, 165
let him go! He's a proper shot: let him vanish! Peace, Jane,
dry up thy tears: they'll make his powder dankish. Take
him, brave men: Hector of Troy was an hackney to him,

148 *pressed* conscripted
148 *set forth* equipped
161 *midriff* ed. (midaffe Q1)
162 *your head* your lord and master
164 *Tawsoone* ed. (Too soone Q1) be quiet
168 *hackney* drudge

---

155 *stand so stiffly . . . newly entered.* Unintentional indecencies.
160 *your polls and your edipolls.* A contracted form of Pollux. Eyre is disparaging Margery's attempt at genteel remonstration: to swear by Pollux is a very mild form of swearing.
163 *and the horns too.* Firk cannot resist the inevitable cuckold joke.

Hercules and Termagant scoundrels; Prince Arthur's
Round Table, by the Lord of Ludgate, ne'er fed such a tall, 170
such a dapper swordman! By the life of Pharaoh, a brave,
resolute swordman! Peace, Jane; I say no more, mad
knaves!

FIRK

See, see, Hodge, how my master raves in commendation of
Ralph! 175

HODGE

Ralph, th'art a gull, by this hand, and thou goest not.

ASKEW

I am glad, good Master Eyre, it is my hap
To meet so resolute a soldier.
Trust me, for your report and love to him,
A common slight regard shall not respect him. 180

LACY

Is thy name Ralph?

RALPH Yes, sir.

LACY Give me thy hand;
Thou shalt not want, as I'm a gentleman.
Woman, be patient; God no doubt will send
Thy husband safe again, but he must go:
His country's quarrel says it shall be so. 185

HODGE

Th'art a gull, by my stirrup, if thou dost not go! I will not
have thee strike thy gimlet into these weak vessels: prick
thine enemies, Ralph!

Enter DODGER

170 *tall* brave
171 *dapper* spruce
176 *gull* simpleton
176 *and* if
176 *not* ed. (om. Q1)
180 *A common slight regard shall not respect him* he shall receive particular
consideration
186 *stirrup* shoemaker's strap for holding the last on his knee
187 *gimlet* boring tool

169 *Termagant.* A fierce heathen god often invoked in the medieval mystery
plays.
170 *Lord of Ludgate.* Possibly the legendary King Lud, whose statue stood
in Ludgate, a city thoroughfare.

DODGER

My Lord, your uncle on the Tower Hill
Stays with the Lord Mayor and the Aldermen,   190
And doth request you with all speed you may
To hasten thither.

ASKEW   Cousin, let us go.

LACY

Dodger, run you before; tell them we come.

Exit DODGER

This Dodger is mine uncle's parasite,
The arrant'st varlet that e'er breathed on earth;   195
He sets more discord in a noble house,
By one day's broaching of his pickthank tales,
Than can be salved again in twenty years;
And he, I fear, shall go with us to France,
To pry into our actions.

ASKEW   Therefore, coz,   200
It shall behove you to be circumspect.

LACY

Fear not, good cousin. Ralph, hie to your colours.

[*Exit* LACY *and* ASKEW]

RALPH

I must, because there is no remedy;
But, gentle master and my loving dame,
As you have always been a friend to me,   205
So in my absence think upon my wife.

JANE

Alas, my Ralph.

MARGERY

She cannot speak for weeping.

190 *Stays* waits
192 *let us* ed. (lets Q1)
    s.d. *Exit* DODGER (Q1 places this stage direction at the end of Dodger's
    speech, 192)
195 *arrant'st varlet* most unmitigated rascal
197 *pickthank* currying favour
201 *behove* benefit
202 *colours* regimental standard
203 *there is* ed. (theres Q1)

---

203 *I must, because there is no remedy*. As a 'serious' character, Ralph speaks
    in blank verse.

EYRE

Peace, you cracked groats, you mustard tokens: disquiet
not the brave soldier. Go thy ways, Ralph.   210

JANE

Ay, ay, you bid him go; what shall I do when he is gone?

FIRK

Why, be doing with me, or my fellow Hodge: be not idle.

EYRE

Let me see thy hand, Jane: this fine hand, this white hand,
these pretty fingers must spin, must card, must work!
Work, you bombast-cotton-candle-quean, work for your   215
living, with a pox to you! Hold thee, Ralph, here's five
sixpences for thee: fight for the honour of the Gentle Craft,
for the gentlemen shoemakers, the courageous cordwainers,
the flower of Saint Martin's, the mad knaves of Bedlam,
Fleet Street, Tower Street and Whitechapel! Crack me the   220
crowns of the French knaves, a pox on them, crack them!
Fight, by the Lord of Ludgate, fight, my fine boy!

FIRK

Here, Ralph, here's three twopences: two carry into France,
the third shall wash our souls at parting, for sorrow is dry.
For my sake, firk the *Basa mon cues*.   225

HODGE

Ralph, I am heavy at parting, but here's a shilling for thee.
God send thee to cram thy slops with French crowns, and
thy enemies' bellies with bullets!

209 *groats* fourpenny coins, here simply a term of jocular abuse
209 *mustard tokens* yellow plague-spots
214 *card* comb or tease the wool
215 *bombast-cotton-candle-quean* bombast is waste cotton such as might be
    used for candle wicks; a quean is a whore: the expression is merely
    boisterous raillery
218 *cordwainers* leather-workers (from Córdoba, in Spain)
224 *wash our souls* i.e., in drink
225 *Basa mon cues* 'baisez mon cul' (kiss my arse): a derisory term for
    Frenchmen
226 *heavy* sad
227 *slops* breeches
227 *French crowns* money, but also an allusion to venereal disease

219 *Saint Martin's*. The parish of St Martin-le-Grand, in which shoemaking
    flourished.
219 *Bedlam*. Bethlehem hospital, a lunatic asylum, outside Bishopsgate.

RALPH

  I thank you, master, and I thank you all.
  Now, gentle wife, my loving lovely Jane,   230
  Rich men at parting give their wives rich gifts,
  Jewels and rings, to grace their lily hands;
  Thou know'st our trade makes rings for women's heels:
  Here, take this pair of shoes cut out by Hodge,
  Stitched by my fellow Firk, seamed by myself,   235
  Made up and pinked with letters for thy name.
  Wear them, my dear Jane, for thy husband's sake,
  And every morning, when thou pull'st them on,
  Remember me, and pray for my return.
  Make much of them, for I have made them so,   240
  That I can know them from a thousand mo.

    Sound drum: enter LORD MAYOR, LINCOLN, LACY, ASKEW,
    DODGER, *and soldiers. They pass over the stage,* RALPH *falls
    in amongst them,* FIRK *and the rest cry farewell, &c., and so
    Exeunt*

[Act I, Scene ii]

Enter ROSE *alone, making a garland*

ROSE

  Here sit thou down upon this flowery bank,
  And make a garland for thy Lacy's head.
  These pinks, these roses, and these violets,
  These blushing gilliflowers, these marigolds,
  The fair embroidery of his coronet,   5
  Carry not half such beauty in their cheeks,
  As the sweet count'nance of my Lacy doth.
  O my most unkind father! O my stars!
  Why loured you so at my nativity,
  To make me love, yet live robbed of my love?   10
  Here as a thief am I imprisoned,
  For my dear Lacy's sake, within those walls
  Which by my father's cost were builded up
  For better purposes; here must I languish

236 *pinked* perforated for eyelets
241 *mo* more

For him that doth as much lament, I know, 15
Mine absence, as for him I pine in woe.

Enter SYBIL

SYBIL
Good morrow, young mistress; I am sure you make that
garland for me, against I shall be Lady of the Harvest.
ROSE
Sybil, what news at London?
SYBIL
None but good: my Lord Mayor your father, and Master 20
Philpot your uncle, and Master Scott your cousin, and
Mistress Frigbottom by Doctors' Commons, do all, by my
troth, send you most hearty commendations.
ROSE
Did Lacy send kind greetings to his love?
SYBIL
O yes, out of cry, by my troth. I scant knew him: here 'a 25
wore a scarf, and here a scarf, here a bunch of feathers, and
here precious stones and jewels, and a pair of garters: O
monstrous! Like one of our yellow silk curtains at home
here in Old Ford House, here in Master Bellymount's
chamber. I stood at our door in Cornhill, looked at him, he 30
at me indeed; spake to him, but he not to me, not a word:
marry gup, thought I, with a wanion! He passed by me as
proud—Marry foh! Are you grown humorous? thought I,
and so shut the door, and in I came.
ROSE
O Sybil, how dost thou my Lacy wrong! 35
My Rowland is as gentle as a lamb,
No dove was ever half so mild as he.

18 *against* for the time when
25 *'a wore a scarf* ed. (a wore scarffe Q1)
32 *marry gup* marry go up, get along with you then
32 *with a wanion* the worse for you
33 *humorous* temperamental

18 *Lady of the Harvest.* The girl elected to preside over the season's
festivities (cf. May-Queen).
22 *Doctors' Commons.* An area near St Paul's, so called because it was
populated by lawyers.

SYBIL

Mild? Yea, as a bushel of stamped crabs! He looked on me
as sour as verjuice: go thy ways, thought I, thou mayest
be much in my gaskins, but nothing in my netherstocks! 40
This is your fault, mistress, to love him that loves not you;
he thinks scorn to do as he's done to, but if I were as you,
I'd cry: Go by, Jeronimo, go by!
I'd set my old debts against my new driblets,
And the hare's foot against the goose giblets, 45
For if ever I sigh when sleep I should take,
Pray God I may lose my maidenhead when I wake!

ROSE

Will my love leave me then and go to France?

SYBIL

I know not that, but I am sure I see him stalk before the
soldiers. By my troth, he is a proper man, but he is proper 50
that proper doth: let him go snick-up, young mistress!

ROSE

Get thee to London, and learn perfectly
Whether my Lacy go to France or no:
Do this, and I will give thee for thy pains
My cambric apron, and my Romish gloves, 55
My purple stockings, and a stomacher.
Say, wilt thou do this, Sybil, for my sake?

SYBIL

Will I, quoth a? At whose suit? By my troth, yes, I'll go:
a cambric apron, gloves, a pair of purple stockings, and a

---

38 *stamped crabs* crab apples crushed to make cider
39 *verjuice* sour juice of unripe fruit
49 *stalk* march
51 *go snick-up* go hang himself
55 *cambric* fine white linen (from Cambray, in Flanders)
56 *stomacher* ornamental chest-covering, often studded with jewels

---

40 *much in my gaskins, but nothing in my netherstocks.* Probably proverbial.
Gaskins were wide breeches, and netherstocks stockings worn under-
neath; hence, 'don't mistake my friendly greeting for anything more
personal'.
43 *Go by, Jeronimo, go by!* A catch-phrase deriving from Kyd's *Spanish
Tragedy*, III. xii, 31, meaning 'have nothing to do with that'.
44 *driblets.* Petty cash. The couplet is proverbial, meaning 'set the good
against the bad and take things as they are'.

stomacher! I'll sweat in purple, mistress, for you; I'll take   60
anything that comes, a God's name! O rich, a cambric
apron! Faith then, have at Up Tails All: I'll go jiggy-joggy
to London and be here in a trice, young mistress.

Exit [SYBIL]

ROSE

Do so, good Sybil; meantime wretched I
Will sit and sigh for his lost company.   65

Exit [ROSE]

[Act I, Scene iii]

Enter ROWLAND LACY *like a Dutch shoemaker*

LACY

How many shapes have gods and kings devised,
Thereby to compass their desired loves!
It is no shame for Rowland Lacy then
To clothe his cunning with the Gentle Craft,
That thus disguised I may unknown possess   5
The only happy presence of my Rose.
For her have I forsook my charge in France,
Incurred the King's displeasure, and stirred up
Rough hatred in mine uncle Lincoln's breast.
O Love, how powerful art thou, that canst change   10
High birth to bareness, and a noble mind
To the mean semblance of a shoemaker!
But thus it must be: for her cruel father,
Hating the single union of our souls,
Hath secretly conveyed my Rose from London   15
To bar me of her presence; but I trust
Fortune and this disguise will further me
Once more to view her beauty, gain her sight.
Here in Tower Street, with Eyre the shoemaker,
Mean I a while to work: I know the trade,   20
I learned it when I was in Wittenberg.

---

62 *Up Tails All.* A catch-phrase from a popular song, meaning 'let's get
   cracking'.
 1 *How many shapes have gods and kings devised.* Lacy justifies his disguise
   by reference to Ovid's tales of metamorphosis.

Then cheer thy hoping spirits, be not dismayed;
Thou canst not want, do Fortune what she can:
The Gentle Craft is living for a man.

Exit [LACY]

[Act I, Scene iv]

Enter EYRE *making himself ready*

EYRE

Where be these boys, these girls, these drabs, these scoundrels? They wallow in the fat brewis of my bounty, and
lick up the crumbs of my table, yet will not rise to see my
walks cleansed. Come out, you powder-beef-queans!
What, Nan! What, Madge Mumblecrust! Come out, you   5
fat midriff-swag-belly whores, and sweep me these kennels,
that the noisome stench offend not the nose of my neigh-
bours. What, Firk, I say! What, Hodge! Open my shop
windows! What, Firk, I say!

Enter FIRK

FIRK

O master, is't you that speak bandog and bedlam this   10
morning? I was in a dream, and mused what madman was
got into the street so early. Have you drunk this morning
that your throat is so clear?

EYRE

Ah, well said, Firk; well said, Firk. To work, my fine
knave, to work! Wash thy face, and thou'lt be more blest.   15

FIRK

Let them wash my face that will eat it; good master, send
for a souse-wife, if you'll have my face cleaner.

Enter HODGE

  s.d. *making himself ready* putting on his dress
  2 *brewis* thick broth
  4 *powder-beef*, salted beef, i.e., cheap meat
  6 *kennels* channels, gutters
  7 *noisome* unpleasant
 10 *bandog and bedlam* roaring like a ferocious watchdog and a lunatic
 17 *souse-wife* woman who pickled pigs' trotters

---

  5 *Madge Mumblecrust.* The rustic crone in Udall's *Ralph Roister Doister.*

EYRE

Away, sloven! Avaunt, scoundrel! Good morrow, Hodge: good morrow, my fine foreman!

HODGE

O master, good morrow; y'are an early stirrer. Here's a 20
fair morning! Good morrow, Firk. I could have slept this hour. Here's a brave day toward!

EYRE

O haste to work, my fine foreman, haste to work!

FIRK

Master, I am as dry as dust to hear my fellow Roger talk of fair weather: let us pray for good leather, and let clowns 25
and ploughboys, and those that work in the fields, pray for brave days. We work in a dry shop; what care I if it rain?

Enter MARGERY

EYRE

How now, Dame Margery, can you see to rise? Trip and go, call up the drabs your maids.

MARGERY

See to rise? I hope 'tis time enough: 'tis early enough for 30
any woman to be seen abroad. I marvel how many wives in Tower Street are up so soon? Gods me, 'tis not noon! Here's a yawling!

EYRE

Peace, Margery, peace. Where's Cicely Bumtrinket your maid? She has a privy fault: she farts in her sleep. Call 35
the quean up: if my men want shoethread, I'll swing her in a stirrup!

FIRK

Yet that's but a dry beating: here's still a sign of drought.

Enter LACY *singing*

LACY

Der was een bore van Gelderland,

25 *clowns* rustics
37 *stirrup* strap (see note on I. i, 186)
39–44 *Der was een bore* . . . 'There was a farmer from Gelderland, /
Merry they are, / He was so drunk he could not stand, / Drunken they
are. / Clink once the cannikin, / Drink pretty mannikin'.

35 *privy*. A pun on 'secret' and 'lavatory'.

 Frolick si byen,   40
He was als dronck he cold nyet stand,
 Upsolce se byen.
Tap eens de canneken,
 Drincke schone mannekin.

FIRK

 Master, for my life, yonder's a brother of the Gentle Craft. 45
If he bear not Saint Hugh's bones, I'll forfeit my bones.
He's some uplandish workman; hire him, good master, that
I may learn some gibble-gabble: 'twill make us work the
faster.

EYRE

 Peace, Firk. A hard world: let him pass, let him vanish! 50
We have a journeyman enow: peace, my fine Firk.

MARGERY

 Nay, nay, y'are best follow your man's counsel; you shall
see what will come on't. We have not men enow, but we must
entertain every butter-box: but let that pass.

HODGE

 Dame, 'fore God, if my master follow your counsel, he'll 55
consume little beef. He shall be glad of men and he can
catch them.

FIRK

 Ay, that he shall!

HODGE

 'Fore God, a proper man, and I warrant a fine workman!
Master, farewell; dame, adieu: if such a man as he cannot 60
find work, Hodge is not for you!   *Offer to go*

EYRE

 Stay, my fine Hodge.

FIRK

 Faith, and your foreman go, dame, you must take a journey
to seek a new journeyman! If Roger remove, Firk follows;
if Saint Hugh's bones shall not be set a-work, I may prick 65

---

44 *schone* ed. (shoue Q1)
47 *uplandish* outlandish, foreign
51 *enow* enough

---

46 *Saint Hugh's bones*. The shoemaker's tools: see Introduction, p. ix.
54 *butter-box* Dutchmen were thought to be prone to gluttony (cf. II. iii,
 141 and IV. iv, 42).

mine awl in the walls and go play! Fare ye well, master;
God buy, dame.

EYRE

Tarry, my fine Hodge, my brisk foreman! Stay, Firk!
Peace, pudding-broth! By the Lord of Ludgate, I love my
men as my life. Peace, you gallimaufry! Hodge, if he want 70
work I'll hire him. One of you to him; stay, he comes to us.

LACY

Goeden dach, meester, ende u vro oak.

FIRK

Nails, if I should speak after him without drinking, I should
choke! And you, friend Oak, are you of the Gentle Craft?

LACY

Yaw, yaw, ik bin den skomawker. 75

FIRK

Den skomaker, quoth a! And hark you, skomaker, have you
all your tools? A good rubbing-pin, a good stopper, a good
dresser, your four sorts of awls and your two balls of wax,
your paring-knife, your hand- and thumb-leathers, and good
Saint Hugh's bones to smooth up your work? 80

LACY

Yaw, yaw; be niet vorveard, ik hab all de dingen voour
mack skoes groot and cleane.

FIRK

Ha, ha! Good master, hire him: he'll make me laugh so
that I shall work more in mirth than I can in earnest.

EYRE

Hear ye, friend: have ye any skill in the mystery of 85
cordwainers?

---

67 *God buy* good-bye (i.e., *God-be-with-you*)
70 *gallimaufry* hotch-potch
72 *Goeden dach, meester, ende u vro oak* 'Good day, master, and to you
mistress also'
73 *Nails* the nails of the Cross, an oath used by Firk again at II. iii, 115
75 *Yaw, yaw, ik bin den skomawker* 'Yes, yes, I am a shoemaker'
75 *bin* ed. (vin Q1)
81 *Yaw, yaw; be niet vorveard* ... 'Yes, yes; be not afraid, I have all the
things for making shoes large and small'

---

86 *cordwainers* see note on I. i, 218.

LACY

Ik weet niet wat yow seg; ich verstaw you niet.

FIRK

Why, thus, man. [*Mimes a shoemaker at work*] Ich verste
u niet, quoth a!

LACY

Yaw, yaw, yaw, ick can dat well doen.   90

FIRK

Yaw, yaw: he speaks yawing like a jackdaw that gapes to
be fed with cheese-curds! O, he'll give a villainous pull at
a can of double-beer! But Hodge and I have the vantage:
we must drink first, because we are the eldest journeymen.

EYRE

What is thy name?   95

LACY

Hans: Hans Meulter.

EYRE

Give me thy hand, th'art welcome! Hodge, entertain him;
Firk, bid him welcome. Come, Hans; run, wife, bid your
maids, your trullibubs, make ready my fine men's breakfasts.
To him, Hodge!   100

HODGE

Hans, th'art welcome. Use thyself friendly, for we are good
fellows; if not, thou shalt be fought with, wert thou bigger
than a giant.

FIRK

Yea, and drunk with, wert thou Gargantua! My master keeps
no cowards, I tell thee! Ho, boy, bring him an heel-block: 105
here's a new journeyman.

Enter Boy

LACY

O ich wersto you: ich moet een halve dossen cans betaelen.

87 *Ik weet niet wat yow seg* . . . 'I know not what you say; I understand you
    not'
87 *verstaw* ed. (vestaw Q1)
90 *Yaw, yaw, yaw, ick can dat wel doen* 'Yes, yes, yes, I can do that well'
99 *trullibubs* trollops
107 *O ich wersto you* . . . 'Oh, I understand you: I must pay for a half dozen
     cans. Here, boy, take this shilling, tap once [i.e., draw a round?] freely'

104 *Gargantua.* The voracious giant in Rabelais's *Gargantua and Pantagruel.*

Here, boy, nempt dis skilling, tap eens freelicke.

Exit Boy

EYRE

Quick, snipper-snapper, away! Firk, scour thy throat, thou
shalt wash it with Castilian liquor. Come, my last of the   110
fives!

Enter Boy

Give me a can: have to thee, Hans; here, Hodge; here, Firk.
Drink, you mad Greeks, and work like true Trojans, and
pray for Simon Eyre the shoemaker! Here, Hans, and
th'art welcome.   115

FIRK

Lo, dame, you would have lost a good fellow that will teach
us to laugh. This beer came hopping in well!

MARGERY

Simon, it is almost seven.

EYRE

Is't so, Dame Clapper-dudgeon? Is't seven o'clock, and my
men's breakfasts not ready? Trip and go, you soused conger, 120
away! Come, you mad Hyperboreans! Follow me, Hodge;
follow me, Hans; come after, my fine Firk: to work, to work
a while, and then to breakfast!   *Exit* [EYRE]

FIRK

Soft! Yaw, yaw, good Hans: though my master have no
more wit but to call you afore me, I am not so foolish to go 125

---

110 *last of the fives* a last for small shoes, i.e., little one

---

s.d. *Exit Boy ... Enter Boy*. The brevity of the interval for fetching
these drinks suggests that Dekker was more concerned to maintain un-
broken the rhythm and pace of the action than with off-stage probability.
Cf. II. iii, 76 and III. iii, 59.

119 *Clapper-dudgeon*. 'A clapperdudgeon is, in English, a beggar born'
(Dekker's *Villainies Discovered*). Steane suggests that Margery's unwelcome interruption of the drinking is being compared to the noise
of the clap-dish by which a beggar attracted attention.

121 *Hyperboreans*. The legendary race of happy folk who were supposed to
live beyond the north wind, out of reach of its blast. Eyre is fond of this
kind of jocular appellation for his workmen, cf. 'mad Greeks' and 'true
Trojans' at 113 above, and 'mad Mesopotamians', II. iii, 78, and 'mad
Cappadocians', V. i, 45.

behind you, I being the elder journeyman.   *Exeunt*

[Act II, Scene i]

Hallooing within. Enter WARNER *and* HAMMON *like hunters*

HAMMON

Cousin, beat every brake, the game's not far:
This way with winged feet he fled from death,
Whilst the pursuing hounds, scenting his steps,
Find out his highway to destruction;
Besides, the miller's boy told me even now   5
He saw him take soil, and he hallooed him,
Affirming him so embossed
That long he could not hold.

WARNER   If it be so,
'Tis best we trace these meadows by Old Ford.
            A noise of hunters within. Enter a Boy

HAMMON

How now, boy, where's the deer? Speak, saw'st thou him? 10

BOY

O yea, I saw him leap through a hedge, and then over a
ditch, then at my Lord Mayor's pale: over he skipped me,
and in he went me, and halloo the hunters cried, and there
boy, there boy! But there he is, 'a mine honesty.

HAMMON

Boy, God amercy; cousin, let's away: 15
I hope we shall find better sport today.

                                    Exeunt

6 *take soil* ed. (take saile Q1) take to watery ground
7 *embossed* foaming at the mouth from exhaustion
12 *pale* fence

126 *the elder journeyman*. Firk has developed a concern for the niceties of
    precedence, now he is no longer the bottom dog. Cf. 'But Hodge and I
    have the vantage: we must drink first' at 93 above, and the processional
    exit at the end of II. iii.

[Act II, Scene ii]

Hunting within. Enter ROSE *and* SYBIL

ROSE

Why, Sybil, wilt thou prove a forester?

SYBIL

Upon some, no! Forester, go by! No, faith, mistress!
The deer came running into the barn, through the orchard,
and over the pale: I wot well, I looked as pale as a new
cheese to see him, but whip! says goodman Pin-close, up   5
with his flail, and our Nick with a prong, and down he
fell, and they upon him, and I upon them. By my troth,
we had such sport! And in the end we ended him, his throat
we cut, flayed him, unhorned him, and my Lord Mayor shall
eat of him anon when he comes.   10

Horns sound within

ROSE

Hark, hark the hunters come: y'are best take heed,
They'll have a saying to you for this deed.

Enter HAMMON, WARNER, *Huntsmen and Boy*

HAMMON

God save you, fair ladies.

SYBIL   Ladies! O gross!

WARNER

Came not a buck this way?

ROSE   No, but two does.

HAMMON

And which way went they? Faith, we'll hunt at those.   15

SYBIL

At those? Upon some, no! When, can you tell?

WARNER

Upon some, ay!

SYBIL   Good Lord!

WARNER   Wounds! Then farewell.

2 *Upon some* goodness me, upon my soul (also at 16 and 17)
4 *wot* know
10 *anon* presently
17 *Wounds* God's wounds, an oath

---

13 *Ladies! O gross!* Davies cites *A Dictionary of the Canting Crew* (*c.* 1700),
which glosses 'lady' as 'a very crooked, deformed and ill shapen woman'.
Sybil deliberately misconstrues Hammon's courtly greeting.

HAMMON
  Boy, which way went he?
BOY   This way, sir, he ran.
HAMMON
  This way he ran indeed; fair Mistress Rose,
  Our game was lately in your orchard seen.   20
WARNER
  Can you advise which way he took his flight?
SYBIL
  Follow your nose: his horns will guide you right.
WARNER
  Th'art a mad wench.
SYBIL   O rich!
ROSE   Trust me, not I.
  It is not like the wild forest deer
  Would come so near to places of resort: 25
  You are deceived, he fled some other way.
WARNER
  Which way, my sugar-candy, can you show?
SYBIL
  Come up, good honeysops; upon some, no.
ROSE
  Why do you stay, and not pursue your game?
SYBIL
  I'll hold my life their hunting nags be lame.   30
HAMMON
  A deer more dear is found within this place.
ROSE
  But not the deer, sir, which you had in chase.
HAMMON
  I chased the deer, but this dear chaseth me.
ROSE
  The strangest hunting that ever I see:
  But where's your park?   *She offers to go away*
HAMMON   'Tis here: O stay!   35

25 *places of resort* frequented places
35 *park* deer-enclosure

---

31 *A deer more dear*. The rhyming stychomythia of this scene turns upon
some well-worn Elizabethan puns relating courtship to hunting.

ROSE

Impale me, and then I will not stray.

WARNER

They wrangle, wench; we are more kind than they.

SYBIL

What kind of hart is that, dear heart, you seek?

WARNER

A hart, dear heart.

SYBIL   Who ever saw the like?

ROSE

To lose your heart, is't possible you can?   40

HAMMON

My heart is lost.

ROSE   Alack, good gentleman!

HAMMON

This poor lost heart would I wish you might find.

ROSE

You by such luck might prove your hart a hind.

HAMMON

Why, Luck had horns, so have I heard some say.

ROSE

Now, God, and't be his will, send luck into your way!   45

Enter LORD MAYOR *and Servants*

LORD MAYOR

What, Master Hammon! Welcome to Old Ford.

SYBIL

God's pittikins, hands off, sir! Here's my Lord!

LORD MAYOR

I hear you had ill luck, and lost your game.

HAMMON

'Tis true, my Lord.

LORD MAYOR   I am sorry for the same.

What gentleman is this?

HAMMON   My brother-in-law.   50

LORD MAYOR

Y'are welcome both; sith Fortune offers you

36 *Impale me* fence me in 51 *sith* since

---

39 *A hart, dear heart.* Another quibble overworked by Elizabethan love
poets. The conventional nature of this verbal game prevents us from
taking Hammon's avowals of love too seriously.

Into my hands, you shall not part from hence
Until you have refreshed your wearied limbs.
Go, Sybil, cover the board; you shall be guest
To no good cheer, but even a hunter's feast.   55

HAMMON

I thank your Lordship. [*Aside*] Cousin, on my life,
For our lost venison I shall find a wife!

Exeunt [*all except* LORD MAYOR]

LORD MAYOR

In, gentlemen: I'll not be absent long.
This Hammon is a proper gentleman:
A citizen by birth, fairly allied.   60
How fit an husband were he for my girl!
Well, I will in, and do the best I can,
To match my daughter to this gentleman.

Exit [LORD MAYOR]

[Act II, Scene iii]

Enter LACY, *Skipper*, HODGE *and* FIRK

SKIPPER

Ick sal yow wat seggen, Hans: dis skip dat comen from
Candy is al wol, by Got's sacrament, van sugar, civet,
almonds, cambric, end alle dingen, towsand towsand ding.
Nempt it, Hans, nempt it vor u meester; daer be de bils
van laden. Your meester Simon Eyre sal hae good copen: 5
wat seggen yow, Hans?

FIRK

Wat seggen de reggen de copen, slopen? Laugh, Hodge,
laugh!

LACY

Mine liever broder Firk, bringt Meester Eyre tot den signe

1 *Ick sal yow wat seggen* . . . 'I shall tell you what, Hans: this ship that
   comes from Candia [i.e., Crete] is all full, by God's sacrament, of sugar,
   civet, almonds, cambric, and all things, a thousand thousand things.
   Take it, Hans, take it for your master; there be the bills of lading. Your
   master Simon Eyre will have a good bargain: what say you, Hans?'
2 *civet* perfume
9 *Mine liever broder Firk* . . . 'My dear brother Firk, bring Master Eyre to
   the sign of the Swan: there shall you find this skipper and me. What say
   you, brother Firk? Do it, Hodge. Come, skipper'

un Swannekin: daer sal yow finde dis skipper end me. Wat   10
seggen yow, broder Firk? Doot it, Hodge. Come, skipper.

Exeunt [LACY *and Skipper*]

FIRK

Bring him, quoth you? Here's no knavery, to bring my
master to buy a ship worth the lading of two or three
hundred thousand pounds! Alas, that's nothing, a trifle, a
bauble, Hodge!   15

HODGE

The truth is, Firk, that the merchant owner of the ship
dares not show his head, and therefore this skipper that
deals for him, for the love he bears to Hans, offers my
master Eyre a bargain in the commodities. He shall have a
reasonable day of payment; he may sell the wares by that   20
time, and be an huge gainer himself.

FIRK

Yea, but can my fellow Hans lend my master twenty
porpentines as an earnest penny?

HODGE

Portuguese, thou would'st say; here they be, Firk: hark,
they jingle in my pocket like Saint Mary Overy's bells.   25

Enter EYRE, MARGERY [*and a Boy*]

FIRK

Mum: here comes my dame and my master. She'll scold,
on my life, for loitering this Monday; but all's one, let them
all say what they can, Monday's our holiday.

15 *bauble* toy, trifle
23 *porpentines* porcupines
23 *earnest penny* down-payment
24 *Portuguese* see note on I. i, 90
25 *Overy's* ed. (Queries Q1)

---

20 *a reasonable day of payment.* Fair time in which to raise the money. As
Davies suggests, Eyre is being given the opportunity to benefit from
what is either a shady business or an Elizabethan trade policy that
discriminated against foreigners. See Introduction, pp. xv–xvi.

24 *Portuguese.* The twenty portuguese which Lacy lends to Eyre are
presumably those he was given by his uncle Lincoln at I. i, 90. Lacy
gave the other ten to Askew at I. i, 107.

25 *Saint Mary Overy.* The church, now the Cathedral of St Saviour, in
Southwark.

MARGERY

You sing, Sir Sauce, but I beshrew your heart;
I fear for this your singing we shall smart.   30

FIRK

Smart for me, dame? Why, dame, why?

HODGE

Master, I hope you'll not suffer my dame to take down
your journeymen.

FIRK

If she take me down, I'll take her up! Yea, and take her
down too, a button-hole lower!   35

EYRE

Peace, Firk! Not I, Hodge! By the life of Pharaoh, by the
Lord of Ludgate, by this beard, every hair whereof I value
at a king's ransom, she shall not meddle with you. Peace,
you bombast-cotton-candle-quean! Away, Queen of Clubs!
Quarrel not with me and my men, with me and my fine Firk: 40
I'll firk you if you do.

MARGERY

Yea, yea, man, you may use me as you please; but let that
pass.

EYRE

Let it pass? Let it vanish away! Peace: am I not Simon
Eyre? Are not these my brave men? Brave shoemakers, all   45
gentleman of the Gentle Craft? Prince am I none, yet am I
nobly born, as being the sole son of a shoemaker. Away,
rubbish! Vanish, melt like kitchen-stuff!

MARGERY

Yea, yea, 'tis well: I must be called rubbish, kitchen-stuff,
for a sort of knaves.   50

---

29 *beshrew* curse
32 *take down* humiliate
47 *sole* (a pun)

---

39 *Queen of Clubs.* Troublemaker (with a pun on the playing card, cf.
V. ii, 30).
46 *Prince am I none, yet am I nobly born.* One of the stories in Deloney's
The Gentle Craft tells 'how the proverb first grew: "A Shoemaker's son
is a prince born"'. W. F. McNeir suggested that Dekker's wording of
Eyre's catch-phrase derives from a line in Greene's *Orlando Furioso*, 'I
am no king, yet am I princely born'.

FIRK

Nay, dame, you shall not weep and wail in woe for me.
Master, I'll stay no longer: here's a venentory of my shop-
tools. Adieu, master; Hodge, farewell.

HODGE

Nay, stay, Firk, thou shalt not go alone.

MARGERY

I pray, let them go; there be mo maids than Mawkin, more   55
men than Hodge, and more fools than Firk.

FIRK

Fools? Nails, if I tarry now, I would my guts might be
turned to shoethread!

HODGE

And if I stay, I pray God I may be turned to a Turk, and
set in Finsbury for boys to shoot at! Come, Firk.   60

EYRE

Stay, my fine knaves, you arms of my trade, you pillars of
my profession. What, shall a tittle-tattle's words make you
forsake Simon Eyre? Avaunt, kitchen-stuff! Rip, you brown-
bread tannikin! Out of my sight, move me not! Have not I
ta'en you from selling tripes in Eastcheap, and set you in   65
my shop, and made you hail-fellow with Simon Eyre the
shoemaker? And now do you deal thus with my journeymen?
Look, you powder-beef-quean, on the face of Hodge:
here's a face for a lord!

FIRK

And here's a face for any lady in Christendom.   70

EYRE

[to Boy] Rip, you chitterling; avaunt, boy: bid the tapster
of the Boar's Head fill me a dozen cans of beer for my
journeymen.

FIRK

A dozen cans? O brave! Hodge, now I'll stay.

---

52 *venentory* Firk's corruption of 'inventory'
55 *mo* more *Mawkin* a slattern (the phrase is proverbial)
64 *tannikin* diminutive form of Anna; cf. 'plain Jane'
71 *chitterling* the edible small-guts of a pig, i.e., 'small fry'

---

72 *Boar's Head.* There were several taverns of this name in Elizabethan
London, including that in Eastcheap celebrated in Shakespeare's
Henry IV.

EYRE

    [*Aside to Boy*] And the knave fills any more than two, he 75
pays for them. [*Exit Boy*] A dozen cans of beer for my
journeymen!

          [*Enter Boy with two cans; puts them down and exit*]

    Hear you, mad Mesopotamians! Wash your livers with this
liquor. Where be the odd ten? No more, Madge, no more.
Well said: drink and to work! What work dost thou, Hodge, 80
what work?

HODGE

    I am making a pair of shoes for my Lord Mayor's daughter,
Mistress Rose.

FIRK

    And I a pair of shoes for Sybil, my Lord's maid: I deal
with her. 85

EYRE

    Sybil? Fie, defile not thy fine workmanly fingers with the
feet of kitchen-stuff and basting-ladles! Ladies of the court,
fine ladies, my lads, commit their feet to our apparelling:
put gross work to Hans. Yark and seam, yark and seam!

FIRK

    For yarking and seaming let me alone, and I come to't. 90

HODGE

    Well, master, all this is from the bias: do you remember
the ship my fellow Hans told you of? The skipper and he
are both drinking at the Swan. Here be the portuguese to
give earnest: if you go through with it, you cannot choose
but be a lord at least. 95

FIRK

    Nay, dame, if my master prove not a lord, and you a lady,
hang me.

89 *Yark* pull the stitches tight
91 *from the bias* off the point (cf. note to I. i, 85)
93 *earnest* down-payment (cf. note to II. iii, 24)

---

    s.d. [*Exit Boy*] . . . [*Enter Boy*]. Q1 gives no stage directions, but the
Boy cannot leave before Eyre's aside to him that only two cans will be
paid for, and he must return before Eyre slily asks after 'the odd ten'.
See note to I. iv, 108.
78 *Mesopotamians*. See note to I. iv, 121. Presumably a quibble on 'mess'
and 'pot' is involved.

MARGERY

Yea, like enough, if you may loiter and tipple thus.

FIRK

Tipple, dame? No, we have been bargaining with Skellum-
Skanderbag-can-you-Dutch-spreaken for a ship of silk   100
Cyprus, lady with sugar-candy.

Enter the Boy with a velvet coat and an alderman's gown.
EYRE *puts it on*

EYRE

Peace, Firk; silence, tittle-tattle. Hodge, I'll go through
with it. Here's a seal-ring, and I have sent for a guarded
gown and a damask cassock—see where it comes! Look
here, Maggy: help me, Firk; apparel me, Hodge. Silk and   105
satin, you mad Philistines, silk and satin!

FIRK

Ha, ha! My master will be as proud as a dog in a doublet,
all in beaten damask and velvet.

EYRE

Softly, Firk, for rearing of the nap, and wearing threadbare
my garments. How dost like me, Firk? How do I look, my   110
fine Hodge?

HODGE

Why, now you look like yourself, master! I warrant you,
there's few in the city, but will give you the wall, and come
upon you with the right-worshipful!

FIRK

Nails, my master looks like a threadbare cloak new turned   115
and dressed. Lord, Lord, to see what good raiment doth!
Dame, dame, are you not enamoured?

103 *guarded* embroidered round the edges
113 *give you the wall* allow you to pass on the inside

---

99 *Skellum-Skanderbag.* As Davies notes, 'Skellum' is probably from the
German 'schelm' ('scoundrel'), while 'Skanderbag' is a corruption of
'Iskander Bey', the Turkish name for a fifteenth-century Albanian
patriot, George Castriot. Here Firk's xenophobic humour equates
'foreigner' and 'rogue' by alliterative association: 'Skanderbag' presumably suggests 'scandal', to echo the word for 'scoundrel'.

100 *silk Cyprus . . . sugar-candy.* Either a confusion or an expansion of the
merchandise as described by the Skipper at II. iii, 1. 'Silk Cyprus' is
black lawn.

EYRE

How sayest thou, Maggy? Am I not brisk? Am I not fine?

MARGERY

Fine? By my troth, sweetheart, very fine! By my troth, I
never liked thee so well in my life, sweetheart! But let that   120
pass: I warrant there be many women in the city have not
such handsome husbands, but only for their apparel: but let
that pass too.

Enter LACY *and Skipper*

LACY

Godden day, mester, dis be de skipper dat heb de skip van
marchandice. De commodity ben good: nempt it, master,   125
nempt it.

EYRE

God amercy, Hans; welcome, skipper. Where lies this ship
of merchandise?

SKIPPER

De skip ben in revere; dor be van sugar, civet, almonds,
cambric, and a towsand towsand tings! Gotz sacrament,   130
nempt it, master: yo sal heb good copen.

FIRK

To him, master, O sweet master! O sweet wares: prunes,
almonds, sugar-candy, carrot-roots, turnips! O brave
fatting meat! Let not a man buy a nutmeg but yourself!

EYRE

Peace, Firk. Come, skipper, I'll go aboard with you. Hans,   135
have you made him drink?

SKIPPER

Yaw, yaw, ic heb veale ge drunck.

---

118 *brisk* smart

s.d. LACY ed. (Hans Q1 and for the remainder of the play in stage directions and speech prefixes)

124 *Godden day, mester* . . . 'Good day, master, this is the skipper that has
the ship of merchandise. The commodity is good: take it, master, take it'

129 *De skip ben in revere* . . . ed. (rovere Q1): 'The ship is in the river; there
is sugar, civet, almonds, cambric, and a thousand thousand things!
God's sacrament, take it, master: you shall have a good bargain'

135 *aboard* ed. (abroade Q1)

137 *Yaw, yaw, ic heb veale ge drunck* 'Yes, yes, I have drunk much'

C

EYRE

> Come, Hans, follow me. Skipper, thou shalt have my
> countenance in the city.

Exeunt [EYRE, LACY *and Skipper*]

FIRK

> Yaw heb veale ge drunck, quoth a. They may well be called   140
> butter-boxes, when they drink fat veal and thick beer too!
> But come, dame, I hope you'll chide us no more.

MARGERY

> No, faith, Firk; no, perdy, Hodge. I do feel honour creep
> upon me, and which is more, a certain rising in my flesh:
> but let that pass.   145

FIRK

> Rising in your flesh do you feel, say you? Ay, you may be
> with child, but why should not my master feel a rising in
> his flesh, having a gown and a gold ring on? But you are
> such a shrew, you'll soon pull him down.

MARGERY

> Ha, ha! Prithee, peace: thou mak'st my worship laugh, but   150
> that pass. Come, I'll go in. Hodge, prithee go before me,
> Firk follow me.

FIRK

> Firk doth follow; Hodge, pass out in state.

Exeunt

[Act II, Scene iv]

Enter LINCOLN *and* DODGER

LINCOLN

> How now, good Dodger, what's the news in France?

DODGER

> My Lord, upon the eighteenth day of May,
> The French and English were prepared to fight;
> Each side with eager fury gave the sign

139 *countenance* support, protection
141 *butter-boxes* see note to I. iv, 54
141 *veal* Firk mistakes the skipper's 'veale'

---

147 *rising in his flesh.* The gown and the gold ring befit a bridegroom as well
as an alderman.

Of a most hot encounter; five long hours   5
Both armies fought together; at the length,
The lot of victory fell on our sides.
Twelve thousand of the Frenchmen that day died,
Four thousand English, and no man of name
But Captain Hyam and young Ardington.   10

LINCOLN

Two gallant gentlemen: I knew them well.
But, Dodger, prithee tell me, in this fight
How did my cousin Lacy bear himself?

DODGER

My Lord, your cousin Lacy was not there.

LINCOLN

Not there?

DODGER   No, my good Lord.

LINCOLN   Sure thou mistakest!   15
I saw him shipped, and a thousand eyes beside
Were witnesses of the farewells which he gave,
When I with weeping eyes bid him adieu.
Dodger, take heed!

DODGER   My Lord, I am advised
That what I spake is true; to prove it so,   20
His cousin Askew that supplied his place
Sent me for him from France, that secretly
He might convey himself hither.

LINCOLN   Is't even so?
Dares he so carelessly venture his life
Upon the indignation of a King?   25
Hath he despised my love, and spurned those favours
Which I with prodigal hand poured on his head?
He shall repent his rashness with his soul;
Since of my love he makes no estimate,
I'll make him wish he had not known my hate!   30
Thou hast no other news?

DODGER   None else, my Lord.

LINCOLN

None worse I know thou hast. Procure the King
To crown his giddy brows with ample honours,

---

11 *Two gallant gentlemen: I knew them well* Q1 gives this as the last line of
   Dodger's speech

Send him chief colonel, and all my hope
Thus to be dashed? But 'tis in vain to grieve: 35
One evil cannot a worse relieve.
Upon my life, I have found out his plot!
That old dog Love that fawned upon him so,
Love to that puling girl, his fair-cheeked Rose,
The Lord Mayor's daughter, hath distracted him;   40
And in the fire of that love's lunacy
Hath he burnt up himself, consumed his credit,
Lost the King's love, yea and I fear, his life,
Only to get a wanton to his wife!
Dodger, it is so.

DODGER   I fear so, my good Lord.   45

LINCOLN
It is so—nay, sure, it cannot be!
I am at my wits' end. Dodger!

DODGER   Yea, my Lord?

LINCOLN
Thou art acquainted with my nephew's haunts:
Spend this gold for thy pains, go seek him out.
Watch at my Lord Mayor's: there, if he live,   50
Dodger, thou shalt be sure to meet with him:
Prithee, be diligent. Lacy, thy name
Lived once in honour, now dead in shame!
Be circumspect.

Exit [LINCOLN]

DODGER   I warrant you, my Lord.

Exit [DODGER]

[Act III, Scene i]

Enter LORD MAYOR *and* MASTER SCOTT

LORD MAYOR
Good Master Scott, I have been bold with you,
To be a witness to a wedding-knot
Betwixt young Master Hammon and my daughter—
O stand aside, see where the lovers come.

Enter HAMMON *and* ROSE

ROSE

   Can it be possible you love me so?   5
   No, no, within those eyeballs I espy
   Apparent likelihoods of flattery.
   Pray now, let go my hand.

HAMMON   Sweet Mistress Rose,

   Misconstrue not my words, nor misconceive
   Of my affection, whose devoted soul   10
   Swears that I love thee dearer than my heart.

ROSE

   As dear as your own heart? I judge it right:
   Men love their hearts best when th'are out of sight.

HAMMON

   I love you, by this hand.

ROSE   Yet hands off now:

   If flesh be frail, how weak and frail's your vow!   15

HAMMON

   Then by my life I swear.

ROSE   Then do not brawl:

   One quarrel loseth wife and life and all.
   Is not your meaning thus?

HAMMON   In faith, you jest.

ROSE

   Love loves to sport: therefore leave love y'are best.

LORD MAYOR

   [*Aside*] What, square they, Master Scott?

SCOTT   [*Aside*] Sir, never doubt.   20

   Lovers are quickly in, and quickly out.

HAMMON

   Sweet Rose, be not so strange in fancying me;
   Nay, never turn aside, shun not my sight.
   I am not grown so fond, to found my love
   On any that shall quit it with disdain: 25
   If you will love me, so; if not, farewell.

LORD MAYOR

   Why, how now, lovers, are you both agreed?

20 *square* quarrel
22 *strange* distant, aloof
24 *fond* foolish
25 *quit* requite

HAMMON

Yes, faith, my Lord.

LORD MAYOR   'Tis well, give me your hand;
Give me yours, daughter. How now, both pull back?
What means this, girl?

ROSE   I mean to live a maid.   30

HAMMON

[*Aside*] But not to die one: pause ere that be said!

LORD MAYOR

Will you still cross me? Still be obstinate?

HAMMON

Nay, chide her not, my Lord, for doing well!
If she can live an happy virgin's life,
'Tis far more blessed than to be a wife.   35

ROSE

Say, sir, I cannot: I have made a vow,
Whoever be my husband, 'tis not you.

LORD MAYOR

Your tongue is quick; but, Master Hammon, know
I bade you welcome to another end.

HAMMON

What, would you have me pule, and pine, and pray,   40
With lovely lady, mistress of my heart,
Pardon your servant, and the rhymer play,
Railing on Cupid and his tyrant's dart?
Or shall I undertake some martial spoil,
Wearing your glove at tourney and at tilt,   45
And tell how many gallants I unhorsed?
Sweet, will this pleasure you?

ROSE   Yea, when wilt thou begin?
What, love-rhymes, man? Fie on that deadly sin!

LORD MAYOR

If you will have her, I'll make her agree.

HAMMON

Enforced love is worse than hate to me.   50

39 *end* purpose, outcome
40 *pule* whine   44 *spoil* conquest

40 *What, would you have me pule, and pine, and pray.* Hammon retrieves
some dignity in defeat by refusing to adopt the poses of the conventional courtly lover.

There is a wench keeps shop in the Old 'Change:
To her will I; it is not wealth I seek;
I have enough, and will prefer her love
Before the world. My good Lord Mayor, adieu:
Old love for me, I have no luck with new.   55

Exit [HAMMON]

LORD MAYOR

Now, mammet, you have well behaved yourself!
But you shall curse your coyness, if I live.
Who's within, there! See you convey your mistress
Straight to th'Old Ford. I'll keep you straight enough!
'Fore God, I would have sworn the puling girl   60
Would willingly accepted Hammon's love;
But banish him my thoughts: go, minion, in!   *Exit* ROSE
Now tell me, Master Scott, would you have thought
That Master Simon Eyre the shoemaker
Had been of wealth to buy such merchandise?   65

SCOTT

'Twas well, my Lord, your Honour and myself
Grew partners with him, for your bills of lading
Show that Eyre's gains in one commodity
Rise at the least to full three thousand pound,
Beside like gain in other merchandise.   70

LORD MAYOR

Well, he shall spend some of his thousands now,
For I have sent for him to the Guildhall.

Enter EYRE

See where he comes. Good morrow, Master Eyre.

EYRE

Poor Simon Eyre, my Lord, your shoemaker.

LORD MAYOR

Well, well, it likes yourself to term you so.   75

Enter DODGER

56 *mammet* doll, little miss

---

51 *the Old 'Change.* The Old Exchange, at the west end of St Paul's.
59 *Old Ford.* A village 3½ miles north-east of St Paul's where the road from
Essex to London formerly forded the River Lea.
63 *Now tell me, Master Scott* ... A very abrupt and awkward shift of
subject. Eyre's brief appearance hardly seems dramatically justified.

Now, Master Dodger, what's the news with you?

DODGER

I'd gladly speak in private to your Honour.

LORD MAYOR

You shall, you shall. Master Eyre and Master Scott,
I have some business with this gentleman:
I pray, let me entreat you to walk before   80
To the Guildhall; I'll follow presently.
Master Eyre, I hope ere noon to call you Sheriff.

EYRE

I would not care, my Lord, if you might call me King of
Spain. Come, Master Scott.

Exeunt [EYRE *and* SCOTT]

LORD MAYOR

Now, Master Dodger, what's the news you bring?   85

DODGER

The Earl of Lincoln by me greets your Lordship,
And earnestly requests you, if you can,
Inform him where his nephew Lacy keeps.

LORD MAYOR

Is not his nephew Lacy now in France?

DODGER

No, I assure your Lordship, but disguised   90
Lurks here in London.

LORD MAYOR   London? Is't even so?
It may be, but upon my faith and soul,
I know not where he lives, or whether he lives.
So tell my Lord of Lincoln. Lurk in London?
Well, Master Dodger, you perhaps may start him;   95
Be but the means to rid him into France,
I'll give you a dozen angels for your pains:
So much I love his Honour, hate his nephew,
And prithee so inform thy lord from me.

DODGER

I take my leave.

LORD MAYOR   Farewell, Master Dodger.   100

Exit DODGER

Lacy in London! I dare pawn my life,

95 *start him* flush him out
97 *angels* a gold coin worth about 50p

My daughter knows thereof, and for that cause
Denied young Master Hammon in his love.
Well, I am glad I sent her to Old Ford.
God's Lord, 'tis late! To Guildhall I must hie: 105
I know my brethren stay my company.

Exit

[Act III, Scene ii]

Enter FIRK, MARGERY, LACY, *and* HODGE

MARGERY

Thou goest too fast for me, Roger. O Firk!

FIRK

Ay, forsooth.

MARGERY

I pray thee run—do you hear?—run to Guildhall and learn
if my husband Master Eyre will take that worshipful voca-
tion of Master Sheriff upon him. Hie thee, good Firk!   5

FIRK

Take it? Well, I go. And he should not take it, Firk swears
to forswear him. Yes, forsooth, I go to Guildhall.

MARGERY

Nay, when? Thou art too compendious and tedious.

FIRK

O rare! Your Excellence is full of eloquence! [*Aside*] How
like a new cart-wheel my dame speaks, and she looks like an   10
old musty ale-bottle going to scalding.

MARGERY

Nay, when? Thou wilt make me melancholy.

FIRK

God forbid your Worship should fall into that humour.
I run!

Exit [FIRK]

MARGERY

Let me see now, Roger and Hans.   15

---

1 *O Firk* ed. (om. Q1)
7 *forswear him* leave him
8 *compendious* succinct, brief (Margery means the opposite)

HODGE

Ay, forsooth, dame—mistress, I should say, but the old term so sticks to the roof of my mouth, I can hardly lick it off.

MARGERY

Even what thou wilt, good Roger: dame is a fair name for any honest Christian, but let that pass. How dost thou, Hans?   20

LACY

Mee tanck you, vro.

MARGERY

Well, Hans and Roger, you see God hath blest your master, and, perdy, if ever he comes to be Master Sheriff of London, as we are all mortal, you shall see I will have some odd thing or other in a corner for you: I will not be your back-   25 friend, but let that pass. Hans, pray thee tie my shoe.

LACY

Yaw, ic sal, vro.

MARGERY

Roger, thou knowest the length of my foot: as it is none of the biggest, so I thank God it is handsome enough. Prithee, let me have a pair of shoes made, cork, good Roger, wooden   30 heel too.

HODGE

You shall.

MARGERY

Art thou acquainted with never a farthingale-maker, nor a French-hood maker? I must enlarge my bum, ha, ha! How shall I look in a hood, I wonder? Perdy, oddly, I think.   35

HODGE

[*Aside*] As a cat out of a pillory—very well, I warrant you, mistress.

21 *Mee tanck you, vro* 'I thank you, mistress'
25 *I will not be your back-friend* I will not let you down (with another, un-intentional, bawdy sense)
27 *Yaw, ic sal, vro* 'Yes, I will, mistress'
35 *Perdy* bless my soul (from 'par dieu')
36 s.p. HODGE ed. (Roger Q1 from here to the end of the scene)

33 *farthingale-maker.* A farthingale was a hooped underskirt to make the lower part of the dress project out from the waist down.
34 *French-hood.* A hood with flaps on either side of the head (hence Hodge's reference to the pillory).

MARGERY

Indeed, all flesh is grass; and Roger, canst thou tell where
I may buy a good hair?

HODGE

Yes, forsooth, at the poulterers in Gracious Street.   40

MARGERY

Thou art an ungracious wag, perdy! I mean a false hair
for my periwig.

HODGE

Why, mistress, the next time I cut my beard you shall have
the shavings of it, but they are all true hairs.

MARGERY

It is very hot: I must get me a fan, or else a mask.   45

HODGE

[*Aside*] So you had need, to hide your wicked face!

MARGERY

Fie upon it, how costly this world's calling is, perdy! But
that it is one of the wonderful works of God, I would not
deal with it. Is not Firk come yet? Hans, be not so sad:
let it pass and vanish, as my husband's Worship says.   50

LACY

Ick bin vrolicke, lot see yow soo.

HODGE

Mistress, will you drink a pipe of tobacco?

MARGERY

O fie upon it, Roger, perdy! These filthy tobacco-pipes are
the most idle slavering baubles that ever I felt. Out upon
it, God bless us, men look not like men that use them!   55

Enter RALPH *being lame*

HODGE

What, fellow Ralph? Mistress, look here: Jane's husband!
Why, how now, lame? Hans, make much of him: he's a
brother of our trade, a good workman, and a tall soldier.

46 *wicked* ugly
51 *Ick bin vrolicke, lot see yow soo* 'I am merry, let me see you so'
58 *tall* brave

---

40 *Gracious Street.* Alternatively Gracechurch Street, leading northwards
    from London Bridge.
52 *drink a pipe of tobacco.* The usual Elizabethan expression.

LACY

You be welcome, broder.

MARGERY

Perdy, I knew him not. How dost thou, good Ralph? I am   60
glad to see thee well.

RALPH

I would God you saw me, dame, as well
As when I went from London into France.

MARGERY

Trust me, I am sorry, Ralph, to see thee impotent. Lord,
how the wars have made him sunburnt! The left leg is not   65
well: 'twas a fair gift of God the infirmity took not hold a
little higher, considering thou camest from France, but let
that pass.

RALPH

I am glad to see you well, and I rejoice
To hear that God hath blest my master so   70
Since my departure.

MARGERY

Yea, truly, Ralph, but let that pass.

HODGE

And, sirrah Ralph, what news, what news in France?

RALPH

Tell me, good Roger, first, what news in England?
How does my Jane? When didst thou see my wife?   75
Where lives my poor heart? She'll be poor indeed,
Now I want limbs to get whereon to feed.

HODGE

Limbs? Hast thou not hands, man? Thou shalt never see
a shoemaker want bread, though he have but three fingers
on a hand.   80

RALPH

Yet all this while I hear not of my Jane!

---

64 *impotent* maimed

---

62 *I would God you saw me, dame, as well.* Ralph speaks in blank verse, as
before.

66 *a little higher.* An allusion to venereal disease, known as 'the French
disease'. Not in the best of taste, but typical of Margery's tactlessness
(assuming it to be intentional).

MARGERY

O Ralph, your wife! Perdy, we know not what's become of
her. She was here a while, and because she was married
grew more stately than became her: I checked her, and so
forth: away she flung, never returned, nor said bye nor   85
bah—and Ralph, you know: ka me, ka thee. And so as I
tell ye. Roger, is not Firk come yet?

HODGE

No, forsooth.

MARGERY

And so indeed we heard not of her; but I hear she lives in
London, but let that pass. If she had wanted, she might   90
have opened her case to me or my husband, or to any of
my men. I am sure there's not any of them, perdy, but
would have done her good to his power. Hans, look if Firk
be come.

LACY

Yaw, ic sal, vro.   95

Exit LACY

MARGERY

And so, as I said: but Ralph, why dost thou weep? Thou
knowest that naked we came out of our mother's womb, and
naked we must return, and therefore thank God for all
things.

HODGE

No, faith, Jane is a stranger here. But Ralph, pull up a   100
good heart: I know thou hast one. Thy wife, man, is in
London: one told me he saw her a while ago, very brave
and neat. We'll ferret her out, and London hold her.

MARGERY

Alas, poor, soul, he's overcome with sorrow. He does but
as I do, weep for the loss of any good thing. But Ralph,   105
get thee in: call for some meat and drink. Thou shalt find
me worshipful towards thee.

84 *stately* ladylike
86 *ka me, ka thee* proverbial expression of mutual help
95 *Yaw, ic sal, vro* 'Yes, I shall, mistress'
95 *ic* ed. (it Q1)   102 *brave* well-dressed   103 *and* if

107 *worshipful.* As bountiful as becomes his Worship the Sheriff's lady.
Margery has not yet learned to use the new title properly.

RALPH

I thank you, dame; since I want limbs and lands,
I'll to God, my good friends, and to these my hands.

Exit [RALPH]

Enter LACY *and* FIRK, *running*

FIRK

Run, good Hans! O Hodge! O mistress! Hodge, heave up   110
thine ears; mistress, smug up your looks, on with your
best apparel! My master is chosen, my master is called—
nay, condemned—by the cry of the country to be Sheriff
of the city, for this famous year now to come, and time
now being. A great many men in black gowns were asked   115
for their voices and their hands, and my master had all their
fists about his ears presently, and they cried Ay, Ay, Ay, Ay,
and so I came away.
Wherefore, without all other grieve,
I do salute you, Mistress Shrieve.   120

LACY

Yaw, my mester is de groot man, de shrieve.

HODGE

Did not I tell you, mistress? Now I may boldly say good
morrow to your Worship.

MARGERY

Good morrow, good Roger; I thank you, my good people
all. Firk, hold up thy hand, here's a threepenny-piece for   125
thy tidings.

FIRK

'Tis but three halfpence, I think. Yes, 'tis threepence, I
smell the rose.

HODGE

But, mistress, be ruled by me and do not speak so pulingly.

111 *smug up* smarten up
112 *condemned* Firk's version of 'confirmed', perhaps
120 *Shrieve* Sheriff
121 *Yaw, my mester is de groot man, de shrieve* 'Yes, my master is the great
    man, the Sheriff'
129 *pulingly* mincingly (cf. 'mealy mouth', I. i, 130)

128 *I smell the rose.* The threepenny-piece bore a profile of Elizabeth wear-
    ing a rose behind her ear. Since this was the coin distributed as maundy-
    money, Margery's largesse here is truly regal, befitting her new sense of
    status.

FIRK

'Tis her Worship speaks so, and not she. No, faith, mistress,   130
speak me in the old key: to it, Firk; there, good Firk; ply
your business, Hodge; Hodge—with a full mouth—I'll fill
your bellies with good cheer 'till they cry twang.

Enter SIMON EYRE *wearing a gold chain*

LACY

See, myn liever broder, heer compt my meester.

MARGERY

Welcome home, Master Shrieve, I pray God continue you   135
in health and wealth.

EYRE

See here, my Maggy, a chain, a gold chain for Simon Eyre!
I shall make thee a lady: here's a French hood for thee.
On with it, on with it, dress thy brows with this flap of a
shoulder of mutton to make thee look lovely. Where be my   140
fine men? Roger, I'll make over my shop and tools to thee;
Firk, thou shalt be the foreman; Hans, thou shalt have an
hundred for twenty. Be as mad knaves as your master
Simon Eyre hath been, and you shall live to be Sheriffs of
London! How dost thou like me, Margery? Prince am I   145
none, yet am I princely born. Firk, Hodge, and Hans!

ALL THREE

Ay, forsooth, what says your Worship, Mistress Sheriff?

EYRE

Worship and honour, you Babylonian knaves, for the Gentle
Craft! But I forget myself: I am bidden by my Lord
Mayor to dinner to Old Ford. He's gone before; I must   150
after. Come, Madge, on with your trinkets! Now, my true
Trojans, my fine Firk, my dapper Hodge, my honest Hans:
some device, some odd crotchets, some morris or suchlike,
for the honour of the gentle shoemakers. Meet me at Old
Ford: you know my mind.   155

---

134 *See, myn liever broder, heer compt my meester* 'See, my dear brothers, here
    comes my master'
149 *forget* ed. (forgot Q1)   153 *crotchets* pranks

---

139 *flap of a shoulder of mutton.* The flap of the French hood (see note to 34
    above), perhaps from a resemblance in shape.
143 *an hundred for twenty.* For the twenty portuguese lent to Eyre by Hans.
153 *morris.* A festive dance in costume.

Come, Madge, away;
Shut up the shop, knaves, and make holiday.

Exeunt [EYRE *and* MARGERY]

FIRK

O rare! O brave! Come, Hodge; follow me, Hans;
We'll be with them for a morris-dance!

Exeunt [FIRK, HODGE, *and* LACY]

[Act III, Scene iii]

Enter LORD MAYOR, EYRE, MARGERY *in a French hood*,
[ROSE,] SYBIL *and other Servants*

LORD MAYOR

Trust me, you are as welcome to Old Ford
As I myself.

MARGERY

Truly, I thank your Lordship.

LORD MAYOR

Would our bad cheer were worth the thanks you give.

EYRE

Good cheer, my Lord Mayor, fine cheer; a fine house, fine   5
walls, all fine and neat.

LORD MAYOR

Now, by my troth, I'll tell thee, Master Eyre,
It does me good, and all my brethren,
That such a madcap fellow as thyself
Is entered into our society.   10

MARGERY

Ay, but, my Lord, he must learn now to put on gravity.

EYRE

Peace, Maggy, a fig for gravity! When I go to Guildhall in
my scarlet gown, I'll look as demurely as a saint, and speak
as gravely as a justice of peace; but now I am here at Old
Ford, at my good Lord Mayor's house, let it go by, vanish,   15
Maggy. I'll be merry: away with flip-flap, these fooleries,
these gulleries! What, honey? Prince am I none, yet am I
princely born. What says my Lord Mayor?

s.d. MARGERY *in a French hood*, [ROSE,] SYBIL . . . ed. (wife, Sibill in a
French hood Q1)

LORD MAYOR

Ha, ha, ha! I had rather than a thousand pound
I had an heart but half so light as yours.   20

EYRE

Why, what should I do, my Lord? A pound of care pays
not a dram of debt. Hum, let's be merry whiles we are
young: old age, sack and sugar, will steal upon us ere we
be aware.

LORD MAYOR

It's well done. Mistress Eyre, pray give good counsel to my   25
daughter.

MARGERY

I hope Mistress Rose will have the grace to take nothing
that's bad.

LORD MAYOR

Pray God she do, for, i'faith, Mistress Eyre,
I would bestow upon that peevish girl   30
A thousand marks more than I mean to give her,
Upon condition she'd be ruled by me.
The ape still crosseth me: there came of late
A proper gentlemen of fair revenues,
Whom gladly I would call son-in-law,   35
But my fine cockney would have none of him.
You'll prove a coxcomb for it, ere you die:
A courtier, or no man, must please your eye.

EYRE

Be ruled, sweet Rose. Th'art ripe for a man: marry not with
a boy that has no more hair on his face than thou hast on thy   40
cheeks. A courtier? Wash, go by, stand not upon pishery-
pashery! Those silken fellows are but painted images; outsides, outsides, Rose: their inner linings are torn. No, my
fine mouse, marry me with a gentleman grocer, like my
Lord Mayor your father. A grocer is a sweet trade, plums,   45
plums! Had I a son or daughter should marry out of the
generation and blood of the shoemakers, he should pack.

36 *my fine cockney* spoiled child   37 *coxcomb* fool
41 *Wash* no more meaning than an expletive, like 'pshaw'
47 *he should pack* he'd have to go

21 *A pound of care pays not a dram of debt.* Proverbial expression included
in *The Oxford Dictionary of English Proverbs*.

What? The Gentle Trade is a living for a man through
Europe, through the world!

A noise within of a tabor and a pipe

LORD MAYOR

What noise is this? 50

EYRE

O my Lord Mayor, a crew of good fellows that for love to
your honour are come hither with a morris-dance. Come in,
my Mesopotamians, cheerily!

Enter HODGE, LACY, RALPH, FIRK, *and other Shoemakers,
in a morris. After a little dancing the* LORD MAYOR *speaks*

LORD MAYOR

Master Eyre, are all these shoemakers?

EYRE

All cordwainers, my good Lord Mayor. 55

ROSE

[*Aside*] How like my Lacy looks yond shoemaker!

LACY

[*Aside*] O that I durst but speak unto my love!

LORD MAYOR

Sybil, go fetch some wine to make these drink;
You are all welcome.

[*Exit* SYBIL]

ALL [THE DANCERS]

We thank your Lordship. 60

[*Enter* SYBIL *with wine*] ROSE *takes a cup of wine and goes
to* LACY

ROSE

For his sake whose fair shape thou represent'st,
Good friend, I drink to thee.

LACY

Ic be dancke, good frister.

MARGERY

I see, Mistress Rose, you do not want judgment: you have
drunk to the properest man I keep. 65

s.d. *tabor* small drum
63 *Ic be dancke, good frister* 'I thank you, good maid'

53 s.d. The first Three-man's Song would be appropriate here after the
dance, or possibly immediately before the shoemakers' exit.

FIRK

Here be some have done their parts to be as proper as he.

LORD MAYOR

Well, urgent business calls me back to London:
Good fellows, first go in and taste our cheer,
And, to make merry as you homeward go,
Spend these two angels in beer at Stratford Bow.   70

EYRE

To these two, my mad lads, Sim Eyre adds another. Then
cheerily, Firk, tickle it, Hans, and all for the honour of
shoemakers.

All go dancing out

LORD MAYOR

Come, Master Eyre, let's have your company.

Exeunt [LORD MAYOR, EYRE *and* MARGERY]

ROSE

Sybil, what shall I do?   75

SYBIL

Why, what's the matter?

ROSE

That Hans the shoemaker is my love Lacy,
Disguised in that attire to find me out.
How should I find the means to speak with him?

SYBIL

What, mistress, never fear; I dare venture my maidenhead   80
to nothing, and that's great odds, that Hans the Dutchman,
when we come to London, shall not only see and speak with
you, but in spite of all your father's policies, steal you away
and marry you. Will not this please you?

ROSE

Do this, and ever be assured of my love.   85

SYBIL

Away then, and follow your father to London, lest your
absence cause him to suspect something.
Tomorrow, if my counsel be obeyed,
I'll bind you prentice to the Gentle Trade.   [*Exeunt*]

72 *tickle it* put some life into it (cf. IV. ii, 7, V. iv, 19)
83 *policies* scheming

---

70 *Stratford Bow*. Stratford-le-Bow in Dekker's time, as in Chaucer's, was
a small village in the country, some 5 miles from St Paul's.

[Act IV, Scene i]

Enter JANE *in a seamster's shop, working, and* HAMMON
muffled, at another door. He stands aloof

HAMMON

Yonder's the shop, and there my fair love sits:
She's fair and lovely, but she is not mine.
O would she were! Thrice have I courted her,
Thrice hath my hand been moistened with her hand,
Whilst my poor famished eyes do feed on that   5
Which made them famish. I am infortunate:
I still love one, yet nobody loves me.
I muse in other men what women see
That I so want? Fine Mistress Rose was coy,
And this too curious—O no, she is chaste!   10
And for she thinks me wanton, she denies
To cheer my cold heart with her sunny eyes.
How prettily she works! O pretty hand!
O happy work! It doth me good to stand
Unseen to see her; thus I oft have stood,   15
In frosty evenings, a light burning by her,
Enduring biting cold, only to eye her.
One only look hath seemed as rich to me
As a king's crown: such is love's lunacy!
Muffled I'll pass along, and by that try   20
Whether she know me.

JANE   Sir, what is't you buy?

What is't you lack, sir? Callico, or lawn?
Fine cambric shirts, or bands? What will you buy?

HAMMON

[*Aside*] That which thou wilt not sell; faith, yet I'll try:
How do you sell this handkercher?

JANE   Good cheap.   25

HAMMON

And how these ruffs?

10 *curious* scrupulous

[*Act IV, Scene i*]. For the Act-division here, see Introduction, p. xxi.
  22 *What is't you lack, sir?* The usual Elizabethan form of crying one's
  wares, here ironically echoing Hammon's own reflection at 8–9.

JANE   Cheap too.

HAMMON   And how this band?

JANE

   Cheap too.

HAMMON   All cheap? How sell you then this hand?

JANE

   My hands are not to be sold.

HAMMON   To be given, then?

   Nay, faith, I come to buy.

JANE   But none knows when.

HAMMON

   Good sweet, leave work a little while: let's play.   30

JANE

   I cannot live by keeping holiday.

HAMMON

   I'll pay you for the time which shall be lost.

JANE

   With me, you shall not be at so much cost.

HAMMON

   Look, how you wound this cloth, so you wound me.

JANE

   It may be so.

HAMMON   'Tis so.

JANE   What remedy?   35

HAMMON

   Nay, faith, you are too coy.

JANE   Let go my hand.

HAMMON

   I will do any task at your command:

   I would let go this beauty, were I not

   Enjoined to disobey you by a power

   That controls kings: I love you.

JANE   So, now part.   40

HAMMON

   With hands I may, but never with my heart.

   In faith, I love you.

JANE   I believe you do.

---

34 *wound this cloth* i.e., with her needle
39 *Enjoined* ed. (In mind Q1)

HAMMON
  Shall a true love in me breed hate in you?
JANE
  I hate you not.
HAMMON   Then you must love.
JANE   I do.
  What, are you better now? I love not you.   45
HAMMON
  All this, I hope, is but a woman's fray
  That means, come to me, when she cries, away.
  In earnest, mistress, I do not jest:
  A true chaste love hath entered in my breast.
  I love you dearly as I love my wife: 50
  I love you as a husband loves a wife.
  That and no other love my love requires;
  Thy wealth I know is little; my desires
  Thirst not for gold; sweet beauteous Jane, what's mine
  Shall, if thou make myself thine, all be thine: 55
  Say, judge, what is thy sentence, life or death?
  Mercy or cruelty lies in thy breath.
JANE
  Good sir, I do believe you love me well,
  For 'tis a silly conquest, silly pride,
  For one like you—I mean a gentleman—   60
  To boast that by his love-tricks he hath brought
  Such and such women to his amorous lure.
  I think you do not so; yet many do,
  And make it even a very trade to woo.
  I could be coy, as many women be,   65
  Feed you with sunshine-smiles and wanton looks;
  But I detest witchcraft. Say that I
  Do constantly believe you constant have—
HAMMON
  Why dost thou not believe me?
JANE   I believe you,
  But yet, good sir, because I will not grieve you   70
  With hopes to taste fruit which will never fall,
  In simple truth this is the sum of all:
  My husband lives, at least I hope he lives.

  46 *a woman's fray* female wrangling

Pressed was he to these bitter wars in France,
Bitter they are to me by wanting him.   75
I have but one heart, and that heart's his due:
How can I then bestow the same on you?
Whilst he lives, his I live, be it ne'er so poor,
And rather be his wife, than a king's whore.

HAMMON

Chaste and dear woman, I will not abuse thee,   80
Although it cost my life if thou refuse me.
Thy husband pressed for France? What was his name?

JANE

Ralph Damport.

HAMMON   Damport? Here's a letter sent
From France to me, from a dear friend of mine,
A gentleman of place: here he doth write   85
Their names that have been slain in every fight.

JANE

I hope Death's scroll contains not my love's name.

HAMMON

Cannot you read?

JANE   I can.

HAMMON   Peruse the same.
To my remembrance such a name I read
Amongst the rest: see here.

JANE   Ay me, he's dead!   90
He's dead; if this be true, my dear heart's slain.

HAMMON

Have patience, dear love.

JANE   Hence, hence.

HAMMON   Nay, sweet Jane,
Make not poor sorrow proud with these rich tears:
I mourn thy husband's death because thou mourn'st.

JANE

That bill is forged: 'tis signed by forgery.   95

HAMMON

I'll bring thee letters sent besides to many,
Carrying the like report: Jane, 'tis too true.
Come, weep not; mourning, though it rise from love,
Helps not the mourned, yet hurts them that mourn.

74 *Pressed* conscripted

JANE

   For God's sake, leave me.

HAMMON   Whither dost thou turn?   100

   Forget the dead, love them that are alive;

   His love is faded, try how mine will thrive.

JANE

   'Tis now no time for me to think on love.

HAMMON

   'Tis now best time for you to think on love,

   Because your love lives not.

JANE   Though he be dead,   105

   My love to him shall not be buried.

   For God's sake, leave me to myself alone.

HAMMON

   'Twould kill my soul to leave thee drowned in moan.

   Answer to my suit, and I am gone:

   Say to me, yea or no.

JANE   No.

HAMMON   Then farewell—   105

   One farewell will not serve: I come again.

   Come, dry these wet cheeks; tell me, faith, sweet Jane,

   Yea or no, once more.

JANE   Once more I say no;

   Once more begone, I pray, else will I go.

HAMMON

   Nay, then, I will grow rude! By this white hand,   110

   Until you change that cold no, here I'll stand,

   Till by your hard heart—

JANE   Nay, for God's love, peace!

   My sorrows by your presence more increase.

   Not that you thus are present, but all grief

   Desires to be alone; therefore in brief   115

   Thus much I say, and saying bid adieu:

   If ever I wed man it shall be you.

HAMMON

   O blessed voice! Dear Jane, I'll urge no more;

   Thy breath hath made me rich.

JANE   Death makes me poor.

                          Exeunt

110 *rude* rough, unmannerly

[Act IV, Scene ii]

Enter HODGE *at his shop-board*, RALPH, FIRK, LACY, *and a Boy at work*

ALL

Hey down a down, down derry.

HODGE

Well said, my hearts! Ply your work today; we loitered yesterday. To it, pell-mell, that we may live to be Lord Mayors, or Aldermen at least.

FIRK

Hey down a down derry!   5

HODGE

Well said, i'faith. How sayest thou, Hans, doth not Firk tickle it?

LACY

Yaw, mester.

FIRK

Not so, neither. My organ pipe squeaks this morning, for want of liquoring. Hey down a down derry!   10

LACY

Forware, Firk, tow best un jolly yongster. Hort I, mester, ic bid yo, cut me un pair vampres vor Mester Jeffrey's bootes.

HODGE

Thou shalt, Hans.

FIRK

Master!   15

HODGE

How now, boy?

---

11 *Forware* ed. (Forward Q1)
11 *Forware, Firk, tow best un jolly yongster* ... 'Indeed, Firk, you are a merry youngster. Hear me, master, I pray you, cut me a pair of vamps for Master Jeffrey's boots'
12 *vampres* ed. (văpres Q1): the front end of the upper shoe

---

1 *Hey down a down, down derry.* The resemblance to the refrain of the second Three-man's Song suggests that it might be sung at the opening of this scene.

FIRK

Pray, now you are in the cutting vein, cut me out a pair of
counterfeits, or else my work will not pass current. Hey
down a down!

HODGE

Tell me, sirs, are my cousin Mistress Priscilla's shoes done?   20

FIRK

Your cousin? No, master, one of your aunts, hang her!
Let them alone.

RALPH

I am in hand with them. She gave charge that none but I
should do them for her.

FIRK

Thou do for her? Then 'twill be a lame doing, and that she   25
loves not. Ralph, thou might'st have sent her to me: in
faith, I would have yerked and firked your Priscilla. Hey
down a down derry! This gear will not hold.

HODGE

How sayest thou, Firk? Were we not merry at Old Ford?

FIRK

How, merry? Why, our buttocks went jiggy-joggy like a   30
quagmire! Well, Sir Roger Oatmeal, if I thought all meal of
that nature, I would eat nothing but bagpuddings.

RALPH

Of all good fortunes, my fellow Hans had the best.

FIRK

'Tis true, because Mistress Rose drank to him.

HODGE

Well, well, work apace; they say seven of the Aldermen   35
be dead, or very sick.

FIRK

I care not; I'll be none.

18 *counterfeits* replacements
21 *aunts* whores
27 *yerked and firked* Firk is in his bawdy vein
28 *gear* way of carrying on
31 *Sir Roger Oatmeal* Sir Roger Otley, the Lord Mayor
32 *bagpuddings* stuffed with a mixture of meat and meal

35 *seven of the Aldermen be dead, or very sick.* An artless preparation for the
news announced by Lacy in IV. iv, 15.

RALPH

No, nor I; but then my master Eyre will come quickly to
be Lord Mayor.

Enter SYBIL

FIRK

Whoop! Yonder comes Sybil.   40

HODGE

Sybil, welcome, i'faith, and how dost thou, mad wench?

FIRK

Sib-whore, welcome to London.

SYBIL

Godamercy, sweet Firk! Good Lord, Hodge, what a
delicious shop you have got! You tickle it, i'faith.

RALPH

Godamercy, Sybil, for our good cheer at Old Ford.   45

SYBIL

That you shall have, Ralph.

FIRK

Nay, by the mass, we had tickling cheer, Sybil. And how
the plague dost thou and Mistress Rose, and my Lord
Mayor? I put the women in first.

SYBIL

Well, Godamercy. But God's me, I forget myself! Where's   50
Hans the Fleming?

FIRK

Hark, butter-box, now you must yelp out some spreken.

LACY

Vat begaie you, vat vod you, frister?

SYBIL

Marry, you must come to my young mistress, to pull on her
shoes you made last.   55

LACY

Vere ben your edle fro, vare ben your mistress?

SYBIL

Marry, here at our London house in Cornwall.

53 *Vat begaie you* . . . 'What do you want, what would you, maid?'
56 *Vere ben your edle fro* . . . 'Where is your noble lady, where is your
mistress?'
57 *Cornwall* Cornhill (cf. I. ii, 30)

FIRK

Will nobody serve her turn but Hans?

SYBIL

No, sir. Come, Hans, I stand upon needles.

HODGE

Why then, Sybil, take heed of pricking!   60

SYBIL

For that let me alone: I have a trick in my budget. Come,
Hans.

LACY

Yaw, yaw, ic sall meete yo gane.

HODGE

Go, Hans; make haste again. Come, who lacks work?

Exit LACY *and* SYBIL

FIRK

I, master, for I lack my breakfast; 'tis munching-time, and   65
past.

HODGE

Is't so? Why then, leave work, Ralph: to breakfast. Boy,
look to the tools; come, Ralph; come, Firk.

Exeunt

[Act IV, Scene iii]

Enter a Servingman

SERVINGMAN

Let me see, now: the sign of the Last in Tower Street.
Mass, yonder's the house! What, haw! Who's within?

Enter RALPH

RALPH

Who calls there? What want you, sir?

SERVINGMAN

Marry, I would have a pair of shoes made for a gentlewoman against tomorrow morning. What, can you do them?   5

61 *a trick in my budget* a gadget in my purse (with a bawdy innuendo)
63 *Yaw, yaw, ic sall meete yo gane* 'Yes, yes, I shall go with you'
64 *make haste again* hurry back
5 *against* by (cf. I. ii, 18)

RALPH

Yes, sir, you shall have them. But what length's her foot?

SERVINGMAN

Why, you must make them in all parts like this shoe, but
at any hand fail not to do them, for the gentlewoman is to
be married very early in the morning.

RALPH

How? By this shoe must it be made? By this? Are you sure,   10
sir? By this?

SERVINGMAN

How? By this? Am I sure? By this? Art thou in thy wits? I
tell thee I must have a pair of shoes, dost thou mark me? A
pair of shoes, two shoes, made by this very shoe, this same
shoe, against tomorrow morning by four o'clock. Dost   15
understand me? Canst thou do't?

RALPH

Yes, sir, yes; ay, ay, I can do't! By this shoe, you say; I
should know this shoe! Yes, sir, yes: by this shoe. I can
do't. Four o'clock, well: whither shall I bring them?

SERVINGMAN

To the sign of the Golden Ball in Watling Street. Enquire   20
for one Master Hammon, a gentleman, my master.

RALPH

Yea, sir. By this shoe, you say.

SERVINGMAN

I say Master Hammon at the Golden Ball. He's the bridegroom, and those shoes are for his bride.

RALPH

They shall be done by this shoe. Well, well, Master   25
Hammon at the Golden Shoe—I would say the Golden
Ball. Very well, very well; but I pray you, sir, where must
Master Hammon be married?

SERVINGMAN

At Saint Faith's Church under Paul's: but what's that to
thee? Prithee, dispatch those shoes, and so farewell.   30

Exit [SERVINGMAN]

8 *at any hand* in any case
29 *Saint Faith's Church under Paul's.* A chapel under the choir of the
    cathedral, used as a parish church by the stationers and others who lived
    in the precincts.

RALPH

By this shoe, said he. How am I amazed
At this strange accident! Upon my life,
This was the very shoe I gave my wife
When I was pressed for France; since when, alas!
I never could hear of her. It is the same,   35
And Hammon's bride no other but my Jane.

Enter FIRK

FIRK

'Snails, Ralph, thou hast lost thy part of three pots a
countryman of mine gave me to breakfast!

RALPH

I care not: I have found a better thing.

FIRK

A thing? Away! Is it a man's thing, or a woman's thing?   40

RALPH

Firk, dost thou know this shoe?

FIRK

No, by my troth, neither doth that know me! I have no
acquaintance with it, 'tis a mere stranger to me.

RALPH

Why then, I do; this shoe, I durst be sworn,
Once covered the instep of my Jane.   45
This is her size, her breadth; thus trod my love;
These true-love knots I pricked; I hold my life,
By this old shoe I shall find out my wife.

FIRK

Ha, ha! Old shoe, that wert new: how a murrain came this
ague-fit of foolishness upon thee?   50

RALPH

Thus, Firk: even now here came a servingman;
By this shoe would he have a new pair made,
Against tomorrow morning, for his mistress
That's to be married to a gentleman.
And why may not this be my sweet Jane?   55

37 *'Snails* God's nails (cf. I. iv, 73)
40 *a man's thing* genital organ (cf. III. ii, 25)
44 *durst* dare
49 *murrain* plague

FIRK

And why mayest not thou be my sweet arse? Ha, ha!

RALPH

Well, laugh, and spare not; but the truth is this:
Against tomorrow morning I'll provide
A lusty crew of honest shoemakers,
To watch the going of the bride to church.   60
If she prove Jane, I'll take her in despite
Of Hammon, and the devil, were he by;
If it be not my Jane, what remedy?
Hereof am I sure: I shall live till I die,
Although I never with a woman lie.   65

Exit [RALPH]

FIRK

Thou lie with a woman, to build nothing but Cripplegates!
Well, God send fools fortune! And it may be he may light
upon his matrimony by such a device, for wedding and
hanging goes by destiny.

Exit [FIRK]

[Act IV, Scene iv]

Enter LACY *and* ROSE, *arm in arm*

LACY

How happy am I by embracing thee!
O I did fear such cross mishaps did reign,
That I should never see my Rose again.

ROSE

Sweet Lacy, since fair Opportunity
Offers herself to further our escape,   5
Let not too over-fond esteem of me
Hinder that happy hour; invent the means,
And Rose will follow thee through all the world.

2 *cross* adverse

---

66 *Cripplegates*. Cripplegate was one of the seven gates in the city walls, so
   called because cripples used to beg there. Firk is making rather a heartless joke about Ralph's lameness.
68 *wedding and hanging goes by destiny*. Cf. *The Merchant of Venice*,
   II. ix, 82–3: 'The ancient saying is no heresy: / Hanging and wiving
   goes by destiny'.

LACY

O how I surfeit with excess of joy,
Made happy by thy rich perfection!   10
But since thou payest sweet interest to my hopes,
Redoubling love on love, let me once more,
Like to a bold-faced debtor, crave of thee
This night to steal abroad, and at Eyre's house,
Who now by death of certain Aldermen   15
Is Mayor of London, and my master once,
Meet thou thy Lacy; where, in spite of change,
Your father's anger, and mine uncle's hate,
Our happy nuptials will we consummate.

Enter SYBIL

SYBIL

O God, what will you do, mistress? Shift for yourself, your   20
father is at hand! He's coming, he's coming! Master Lacy,
hide yourself! In, my mistress! For God's sake, shift for
yourselves!

LACY

Your father come! Sweet Rose, what shall I do?
Where shall I hide me? How shall I escape?   25

ROSE

A man, and want wit in extremity?
Come, come, be Hans still: play the shoemaker,
Pull on my shoe.

Enter LORD MAYOR

LACY

Mass, and that's well remembered!

SYBIL

Here comes your father.   30

LACY

Forware, metresse, tis un good skow; it sal vel dute, or ye

19 *we* ed. (me Q1)
31 *Forware, metresse, tis un good skow* ... 'Indeed, mistress, it is a good
shoe; it shall do well, or you shall not pay for it'

---

15 *Who now by death of certain Aldermen | Is Mayor of London.* Not un-
expected news (cf. IV. ii, 38), but slipped in very casually here.
22 *Master Lacy, hide yourself! In, my mistress!* The punctuation represents
what Sybil means to say; 'hide your selfe in my mistris' (Q1), however,
suggests that the line may be played for a bawdy laugh.

sal neit betallen.

ROSE

O God, it pincheth me! What will you do?

LACY

Your father's presence pincheth, not the shoe.

LORD MAYOR

Well done; fit my daughter well, and she shall please thee   35
well.

LACY

Yaw, yaw, ick weit dat well. Forware tis un good skoo, tis
gi mait van neits leither: se ever, mine here.

Enter a Prentice

LORD MAYOR

I do believe it. What's the news with you?

PRENTICE

Please you, the Earl of Lincoln at the gate   40
Is newly lighted, and would speak with you.

LORD MAYOR

The Earl of Lincoln come to speak with me?
Well, well, I know his errand. Daughter Rose,
Send hence your shoemaker: dispatch, have done!
Sib, make things handsome! Sir boy, follow me.   45
            Exit [LORD MAYOR, SYBIL *and Prentice*]

LACY

Mine uncle come? O what may this portend?
Sweet Rose, this of our love threatens an end.

ROSE

Be not dismayed at this: whate'er befall,
Rose is thine own. To witness I speak truth,
Where thou appoints the place I'll meet with thee.   50
I will not fix a day to follow thee,
But presently steal hence. Do not reply:

---

37 *Yaw, yaw, ick weit dat well* . . . 'Yes, yes, I know that well. Indeed it is a
    good shoe, it is made of neat's leather: just see, my lord'
42 *to* ed. (om. Q1)
52 *presently* immediately

---

35 *fit my daughter well, and she shall please thee well.* Another unintentional
    indecency.

D

Love which gave strength to bear my father's hate,
Shall now add wings to further our escape.

Exeunt

[Act IV, Scene v]

Enter LORD MAYOR *and* LINCOLN

LORD MAYOR
  Believe me, on my credit I speak truth,
  Since first your nephew Lacy went to France
  I have not seen him. It seemed strange to me,
  When Dodger told me that he stayed behind,
  Neglecting the high charge the King imposed. 5
LINCOLN
  Trust me, Sir Roger Otley, I did think
  Your counsel had given head to this attempt,
  Drawn to it by the love he bears your child.
  Here I did hope to find him in your house,
  But now I see mine error, and confess 10
  My judgment wronged you by conceiving so.
LORD MAYOR
  Lodge in my house, say you? Trust me, my Lord,
  I love your nephew Lacy too too dearly
  So much to wrong his honour, and he hath done so,
  That first gave him advice to stay from France. 15
  To witness I speak truth, I let you know
  How careful I have been to keep my daughter
  Free from all conference or speech of him.
  Not that I scorn your nephew, but in love
  I bear your honour, lest your noble blood 20
  Should by my mean worth be dishonoured.
LINCOLN
  [*Aside*] How far the churl's tongue wanders from his heart!
  Well, well, Sir Roger Otley, I believe you,
  With more than many thanks for the kind love
  So much you seem to bear me; but, my Lord, 25
  Let me request your help to seek my nephew,
  Whom, if I find, I'll straight embark for France.

7 *given head* encouraged

So shall your Rose be free, my thoughts at rest,
And much care die which now lies in my breast.

Enter SYBIL

SYBIL

O Lord! Help, for God's sake! My mistress, O my young   30
mistress!

LORD MAYOR

Where is thy mistress? What's become of her?

SYBIL

She's gone, she's fled!

LORD MAYOR

Gone? Whither is she fled?

SYBIL

I know not, forsooth. She's fled out of doors with Hans the   35
shoemaker. I saw them scud, scud, scud, apace, apace!

LORD MAYOR

Which way? What, John! Where be my men? Which way?

SYBIL

I know not, and it please your Worship.

LORD MAYOR

Fled with a shoemaker? Can this be true?

SYBIL

O Lord, sir, as true as God's in heaven!   40

LINCOLN

[*Aside*] Her love turned shoemaker? I am glad of this!

LORD MAYOR

A Fleming butter-box? A shoemaker?
Will she forget her birth? Requite my care
With such ingratitude? Scorned she young Hammon,
To love a honnikin, a needy knave?   45
Well, let her fly, I'll not fly after her.
Let her starve if she will, she's none of mine!

LINCOLN

Be not so cruel, sir.

Enter FIRK *with shoes*

---

28 *your Rose . . . my thoughts* ed. (my Rose . . . your thoughts Q1)
29 *lies* ed. (dies Q1)
45 *honnikin* contemptuous term for a Dutchman or German ('little Hun'?)

SYBIL

[*Aside*] I am glad she's 'scaped.

LORD MAYOR

I'll not account of her as of my child! 50
Was there no better object for her eyes,
But a foul, drunken lubber, swill-belly?
A shoemaker? That's brave!

FIRK

Yea, forsooth, 'tis a very brave shoe, and as fit as a pudding.

LORD MAYOR

How now, what knave is this? From whence comest thou? 55

FIRK

No knave, sir. I am Firk the shoemaker, lusty Roger's chief
lusty journeyman, and I come hither to take up the pretty
leg of sweet Mistress Rose, and thus hoping your Worship
is in good health as I was at the making hereof, I bid you
farewell, yours, Firk. 60

[*Starts to leave*]

LORD MAYOR

Stay, stay, sir knave!

LINCOLN

Come hither, shoemaker.

FIRK

'Tis happy the knave is put before the shoemaker, or else
I would not have vouchsafed to come back to you. I am
moved, for I stir. 65

LORD MAYOR

My Lord, this villain calls us knaves by craft!

FIRK

Then 'tis by the Gentle Craft, and to call one knave gently
is no harm. Sit your Worship merry! [*Aside*] Sib, your
young mistress! I'll so bob them, now my master, Master
Eyre, is Lord Mayor of London! 70

53 *That's brave* That's wonderful (ironic)
64 *vouchsafed* guaranteed
69 *bob them* ed. (bob then Q1) fool them

56 *No knave, sir.* Firk defends the dignity of the Gentle Craft in dealing
with the Lord Mayor's overbearing manner. His chief purpose in this
scene, of course, is to cover the retreat of Rose and Lacy, by playing for
time and then misleading the Lord Mayor and Lincoln.

LORD MAYOR

Tell me, sirrah, whose man are you?

FIRK

I am glad to see your Worship so merry. I have no maw
to this gear, no stomach as yet to a red petticoat.

Pointing to SYBIL

LINCOLN

He means not, sir, to woo you to this maid,

But only doth demand whose man you are.   75

FIRK

I sing now to the tune of Rogero: Roger, my fellow, is now
my master.

LINCOLN

Sirrah, knowest thou one Hans, a shoemaker?

FIRK

Hans, shoemaker? O yes; stay, yes, I have him! I tell you
what, I speak it in secret: Mistress Rose and he are by this   80
time—no, not so, but shortly are to come over one another
with 'Can you dance the shaking of the sheets?' It is that
Hans. [*Aside*] I'll so gull these diggers!

LORD MAYOR

Knowest thou then where he is?

FIRK

Yes, forsooth: yea, marry.   85

LINCOLN

Canst thou, in sadness?

FIRK

No, forsooth: no, marry.

LORD MAYOR

Tell me, good honest fellow, where he is,

And thou shalt see what I'll bestow of thee.

FIRK

Honest fellow? No, sir; not so, sir. My profession is the   90
Gentle Craft: I care not for seeing, I love feeling. Let me

72 *no maw to this gear* no appetite for this kind of game
76 *the tune of Rogero* a popular Elizabethan tune
82 *the shaking of the sheets* the name of an old dance, with an obvious sexual
allusion (cf. V. v, 29)
83 *gull these diggers* fool them for trying to dig information out of me
86 *sadness* seriousness

feel it here, *aurium tenus*, ten pieces of gold, *genuum tenus*, ten pieces of silver, and then Firk is your man, in a new pair of stretchers.

LORD MAYOR

Here is an angel, part of thy reward   95
Which I will give thee: tell me where he is.

FIRK

No point! Shall I betray my brother? No! Shall I prove Judas to Hans? No! Shall I cry treason to my corporation? No! I shall be firked and yerked then. But give me your angel: your angel shall tell you.   100

LINCOLN

Do so, good fellow, 'tis no hurt to thee.

FIRK

Send simpering Sib away.

LORD MAYOR

Huswife, get you in.

Exit SYBIL

FIRK

Pitchers have ears, and maids have wide mouths. But for Hans-prans, upon my word, tomorrow morning he and   105
young Mistress Rose go to this gear; they shall be married together, by this rush, or else turn Firk to a firkin of butter to tan leather withal.

LORD MAYOR

But art thou sure of this?

FIRK

Am I sure that Paul's steeple is a handful higher than   110

---

94 *stretchers* shoe-stretchers, here also truth-stretchers
97 *No point* Absolutely not
98 *corporation* fellow-shoemakers
99 *firked and yerked* worked over (cf. IV. ii, 27)

---

92 *aurium tenus . . . genuum tenus*. 'As far as the ears . . . as far as the knees', i.e., gold for the whole truth, silver for part of the truth, with puns on 'aurium' (gold) and 'tenus' (ten).
107 *by this rush*. Rushes were used as floor-coverings, but a rush-ring was said to be used by bridegrooms not intending to keep their vows; so here Firk equivocates in swearing that he tells the truth.

London Stone? Or that the pissing-conduit leaks nothing
but pure Mother Bunch? Am I sure I am lusty Firk? God's
nails, do you think I am so base to gull you?

LINCOLN

Where are they married? Dost thou know the church?

FIRK

I never go to church, but I know the name of it. It is a   115
swearing-church: stay a while, 'tis Ay-by-the-mass; no, no,
'tis Ay-by-my-troth; no, nor that, 'tis Ay-by-my-faith.
That, that! 'Tis Ay-by-my-Faith's Church under Paul's
Cross: there they shall be knit, like a pair of stockings, in
matrimony; there they'll be in cony.   120

LINCOLN

Upon my life, my nephew Lacy walks
In the disguise of this Dutch shoemaker!

FIRK

Yes, forsooth.

LINCOLN

Doth he not, honest fellow?

FIRK

No, forsooth. I think Hans is nobody but Hans, no spirit.   125

LORD MAYOR

My mind misgives me now 'tis so indeed!

LINCOLN

My cousin speaks the language, knows the trade.

LORD MAYOR

Let me request your company, my Lord.
Your honourable presence may, no doubt,
Refrain their headstrong rashness, when myself   130
Going alone perchance may be o'erborne.
Shall I request this favour?

LINCOLN   This, or what else.

120 *in cony* set up nicely

---

111 *London Stone*. It marked the converging-point of the old Roman roads.
111 *pissing-conduit*. A water-cistern near the Royal Exchange, probably so
called because it leaked. Steane cites Jack Cade in *Henry VI*, IV. vi, 3:
'And here sitting upon London Stone, I charge and command that, of
the City's cost, the pissing conduit run nothing but claret wine this first
of my reign'.
112 *Mother Bunch*. An ale-wife notorious for watering her beer.

FIRK

   Then you must rise betimes, for they mean to fall to their
hey-pass-and-repass, pindy-pandy, which-hand-will-you-
have very early.   135

LORD MAYOR

   My care shall every way equal their haste.
[*To* LINCOLN] This night accept your lodging in my house;
The earlier shall we stir, and at Saint Faith's
Prevent this giddy harebrained nuptial;
This traffic of hot love shall yield cold gains: 140
They ban our loves, and we'll forbid their banns.

                             [*Exit* LORD MAYOR]

LINCOLN

   At Saint Faith's Church, thou sayest?

FIRK

   Yes, by their troth.

LINCOLN

   Be secret, on thy life!   [*Exit* LINCOLN]

FIRK

   Yes, when I kiss your wife! Ha, ha! Here's no craft in the   145
Gentle Craft: I came hither of purpose with shoes to Sir
Roger's Worship, whilst Rose his daughter be conycatched
by Hans. Soft now! These two gulls will be at Saint Faith's
Church tomorrow morning, to take Master Bridegroom
and Mistress Bride napping, and they in the meantime shall   150
chop up the matter at the Savoy! But the best sport is, Sir
Roger Otley will find my fellow lame Ralph's wife going to
marry a gentleman, and then he'll stop her instead of his
daughter! O brave, there will be fine tickling sport! Soft now,
what have I to do? O I know now: a mess of shoemakers   155
meet at the Woolsack in Ivy Lane, to cozen my gentleman

---

134 *hey-pass-and-repass* a conjuring term: 'artful tricks'
134 *pindy-pandy* handy-dandy, i.e., giving of hands in marriage
    s.d. *Exit* [LORD MAYOR] ed. (Exeunt Q1)
    s.d. [*Exit* LINCOLN] ed. (om. Q1)
147 *conycatched* caught by a trick
151 *chop up* swiftly conclude
156 *cozen* cheat

---

151 *the Savoy.* A paupers' hospital the chapel of which was frequently used
    for clandestine marriages.

of lame Ralph's wife, that's true.
Alack, alack!
Girls, hold out tack!
For now smocks for this jumbling   160
Shall go to wrack.

Exit [FIRK]

[Act V, Scene i]

Enter EYRE, MARGERY, LACY, *and* ROSE

EYRE

This is the morning then, stay, my bully, my honest Hans,
is it not?

LACY

This is the morning that must make us two
Happy or miserable; therefore, if you—

EYRE

Away with these ifs and ands, Hans, and these etceteras!   5
By mine honour, Rowland Lacy, none but the King shall
wrong thee! Come, fear nothing: am not I Sim Eyre? Is
not Sim Eyre Lord Mayor of London? Fear nothing, Rose,
let them all say what they can. 'Dainty, come thou to me':
laughest thou?   10

MARGERY

Good my Lord, stand her friend in what thing you may.

EYRE

Why, my sweet Lady Madgy, think you Simon Eyre can
forget his fine Dutch journeyman? No, vah! Fie, I scorn
it! It shall never be cast in my teeth that I was unthankful.
Lady Madgy, thou hadst never covered thy saracen's head   15
with this French flap, nor loaden thy bum with this farthing-
gale—'tis trash, trumpery, vanity!—Simon Eyre had never
walked in a red petticoat, nor wore a chain of gold, but for
my fine journeyman's portuguese: and shall I leave him?

159 *hold out tack* be on your guard
160 *smocks* maidenhoods *jumbling* confusion
  1 *stay, my bully* now, my fine fellow
  9 *'Dainty, come thou to me'* the opening of a popular song

11 *stand her friend in what thing you may.* Another example of Margery's
habit of unintentional *double-entendre* (cf. V. ii, 159).

No! Prince am I none, yet bear a princely mind.   20

LACY

My Lord, 'tis time for us to part from hence.

EYRE

Lady Madgy, Lady Madgy, take two or three of my
piecrust-eaters, my buff-jerkin varlets, that do walk in black
gowns at Simon Eyre's heels. Take them, good Lady
Madgy. Trip and go, my brown queen of periwigs, with my   25
delicate Rose and my jolly Rowland to the Savoy; see them
linked, countenance the marriage, and when it is done,
cling, cling together, you Hamborow turtle-doves! I'll bear
you out! Come to Simon Eyre, come dwell with me, Hans.
Thou shalt eat minced pies and marchpane. Rose, away,   30
cricket! Trip and go, my Lady Madgy, to the Savoy! Hans,
wed and to bed! Kiss and away, go, vanish!

MARGERY

Farewell, my Lord.

ROSE

Make haste, sweet love.

MARGERY

She'd fain the deed were done.   35

LACY

Come, my sweet Rose, faster than deer we'll run!

They go out

EYRE

Go, vanish, vanish, avaunt, I say! By the Lord of Ludgate,
it's a mad life to be a Lord Mayor, it's a stirring life, a fine
life, a velvet life, a careful life! Well, Simon Eyre, yet set
a good face on it, in the honour of Saint Hugh. Soft! The   40
King this day comes to dine with me, to see my new build-
ings: His Majesty is welcome, he shall have good cheer,
delicate cheer, princely cheer. This day my fellow prentices
of London come to dine with me too: they shall have fine
cheer, gentlemanlike cheer. I promised the mad Cappadoc-   45

---

27 *countenance* witness   30 *marchpane* marzipan

---

45 *mad Cappadocians.* Another of Eyre's jocular appellations (cf. 'mad
    Greeks', I. iv, 113, 'mad Hyperboreans', I. iv, 121, and 'mad Meso-
    potamians', II. iii, 78). Here possibly with a pun on 'madcaps' and
    bearing the cant association with imprisonment: N.E.D. cites 'Caper-
    dewsie' and 'Caperdochy' as terms for prison and the stocks.

ians, when we all served at the Conduit together, that if
ever I came to be Mayor of London I would feast them all,
and I'll do't, I'll do't, by the life of Pharoah! By this beard,
Sim Eyre will be no flincher! Besides, I have procured that
upon every Shrove Tuesday, at the sound of the pancake   50
bell, my fine dapper Assyrian lads shall clap up their shop
windows, and away. This is the day, and this day they shall
do't, they shall do't!
Boys, that day are you free: let masters care,
And prentices shall pray for Simon Eyre.   55

Exit

[Act V, Scene ii]

Enter HODGE, FIRK, RALPH, *and five or six shoemakers, all
with cudgels or such weapons*

HODGE

Come, Ralph; stand to it, Firk. My masters, as we are the
brave bloods of the shoemakers, heirs apparent to Saint
Hugh, and perpetual benefactors to all good fellows, thou
shalt have no wrong. Were Hammon a King of Spades, he
should not delve in thy close without thy sufferance! But   5
tell me, Ralph, art thou sure 'tis thy wife?

RALPH

Am I sure this is Firk? This morning, when I stroked on
her shoes, I looked upon her, and she upon me, and sighed,
asked me if ever I knew one Ralph. Yes, said I; for his
sake, said she, tears standing in her eyes, and for thou art   10
somewhat like him, spend this piece of gold. I took it: my
lame leg, and my travel beyond sea, made me unknown. All
is one for that: I know she's mine.

4 *King of Spades* pun on 'spades': cf. 'Queen of Clubs', II. iii, 39
5 *delve in thy close* dig in your patch
5 *sufferance* permission

---

46 *served at the Conduit.* Alluding to the customary duty of apprentices to
fetch the water for their masters' houses.
50 *every Shrove Tuesday.* The traditional apprentices' holiday, being the
day before the beginning of Lent. See Introduction, p. xiii.
50 *the pancake bell.* Originally a summons to confession before Lent, but
in popular tradition the signal to commence the Shrove Tuesday
festivities.

FIRK

Did she give thee this gold? O glorious glittering gold!
She's thine own, 'tis thy wife, and she loves thee, for I'll   15
stand to't, there's no woman will give gold to any man but
she thinks better of him than she thinks of them she gives
silver to. And for Hammon, neither Hammon nor hangman
shall wrong thee in London. Is not our old master Eyre
Lord Mayor? Speak, my hearts!   20

ALL

Yes, and Hammon shall know it to his cost.

Enter HAMMON, *his Man,* JANE, *and others*

HODGE

Peace, my bullies, yonder they come.

RALPH

Stand to't, my hearts! Firk, let me speak first.

HODGE

No, Ralph, let me. Hammon, whither away so early?

HAMMON

Unmannerly rude slave, what's that to thee?   25

FIRK

To him, sir? Yes, sir, and to me, and others! Good morrow,
Jane, how dost thou? Good Lord, how the world is changed
with you, God be thanked!

HAMMON

Villains, hands off! How dare you touch my love?

ALL

Villains? Down with them! Cry clubs for prentices!   30

HODGE

Hold, my hearts! Touch her, Hammon? Yea, and more than
that: we'll carry her away with us. My masters and gentlemen, never draw your bird-spits: shoemakers are steel to
the back, men every inch of them, all spirit.

33 *bird-spits* contemptuous term for daggers and swords

---

18 *neither Hammon nor hangman.* A play on the name, with an allusion to the
Biblical King Haman (in the Book of Esther) who was hanged on his
own gallows.

30 *Cry clubs for prentices.* The rallying cry that brought the apprentices out
on the streets for a gang-fight (and possibly with a reference back to
Hammon as 'King of Spades' at 4 above?).

ALL OF HAMMON'S SIDE

　Well, and what of all this?　　　　　　　　　　　　35

HODGE

　I'll show you. Jane, dost thou know this man? 'Tis Ralph,
　I can tell thee. Nay, 'tis he, in faith; though he be lamed
　by the wars, yet look not strange, but run to him, fold him
　about the neck and kiss him!

JANE

　Lives then my husband? O God, let me go!　　　　40
　Let me embrace my Ralph.

HAMMON　　　　　　　　　What means my Jane?

JANE

　Nay, what meant you, to tell me he was slain?

HAMMON

　Pardon me, dear love, for being misled.
　[To RALPH] 'Twas rumoured here in London thou wert dead.

FIRK

　Thou seest he lives. Lass, go pack home with him. Now,　45
　Master Hammon, where's your mistress, your wife?

SERVINGMAN

　'Swounds, master, fight for her! Will you thus lose her?

ALL [OF RALPH'S SIDE]

　Down with that creature! Clubs, down with him!

HODGE

　Hold, hold!

HAMMON

　Hold, fool! Sirs, he shall do no wrong.　　　　　　50
　Will my Jane leave me thus, and break her faith?

FIRK

　Yea, sir; she must, sir; she shall, sir! What then? Mend it.

HODGE

　Hark, fellow Ralph, follow my counsel. Set the wench in
　the midst, and let her choose her man, and let her be his
　woman.　　　　　　　　　　　　　　　　　　55

JANE

　Whom should I choose? Whom should my thoughts affect,
　But him whom Heaven hath made to be my love!
　Thou art my husband, and these humble weeds
　Makes thee more beautiful than all his wealth.
　Therefore I will but put off his attire,　　　　　60
　Returning it into the owner's hand,

And after ever be thy constant wife.

HODGE

Not a rag, Jane! The law's on our side: he that sows in
another man's ground forfeits his harvest. Get thee home,
Ralph; follow him, Jane. He shall not have so much as a   65
busk-point from thee.

FIRK

Stand to that, Ralph, the appurtenances are thine own.
Hammon, look not at her.

SERVINGMAN

O 'swounds! No!

FIRK

Blue coat, be quiet: we'll give you a new livery else! We'll   70
make Shrove Tuesday Saint George's Day for you! Look
not, Hammon, leer not! I'll firk you! For thy head now:
one glance, one sheep's eye, anything, at her! Touch not a
rag, lest I and my brethren beat you to clouts!

SERVINGMAN

Come, Master Hammon, there's no striving here.   75

HAMMON

Good fellows, hear me speak; and honest Ralph,
Whom I have injured most by loving Jane,
Mark what I offer thee: here in fair gold
Is twenty pound, I'll give it for thy Jane.
If this content thee not, thou shalt have more.   80

HODGE

Sell not thy wife, Ralph, make her not a whore.

HAMMON

Say, wilt thou freely cease thy claim in her,
And let her be my wife?

ALL [OF RALPH'S SIDE]   No, do not, Ralph!

RALPH

Sirrah Hammon, Hammon, dost thou think a shoemaker
is so base, to be a bawd to his own wife for commodity?   85

66 *busk-point* corset-lace
74 *clouts* rags
75 *striving* quarrelling
85 *commodity* profit

71 *Saint George's Day.* When servants might change or renew their terms
of service, i.e., Firk is threatening to beat him black and blue.

Take thy gold, choke with it! Were I not lame, I would
make thee eat thy words!

FIRK

A shoemaker sell his flesh and blood? O indignity!

HODGE

Sirrah, take your pelf and be packing.

HAMMON

I will not touch one penny; but in lieu   90
Of that great wrong I offered thy Jane,
To Jane and thee I give that twenty pound.
Since I have failed of her, during my life
I vow no woman else shall be my wife.
Farewell, good fellows of the Gentle Trade: 95
Your morning's mirth my mourning-day hath made.

                    Exeunt [HAMMON *and those of his side*]

FIRK

[*To Servingman going out*] Touch the gold, creature, if you
dare! Y'are best be trudging! Here, Jane, take thou it.
Now let's home, my hearts!

HODGE

Stay, who comes here? Jane, on again with thy mask.   100

                Enter LINCOLN, LORD MAYOR, *and Servants*

LINCOLN

Yonder's the lying varlet mocked us so!

LORD MAYOR

Come hither, sirrah.

FIRK

Ay, sir, I am sirrah: you mean me, do you not?

LINCOLN

Where is my nephew married?

FIRK

Is he married? God give him joy, I am glad of it. They   105
have a fair day, and the sign is in a good planet: Mars in
Venus.

89 *pelf* money

---

96 *Your morning's mirth my mourning-day hath made.* The unfortunate
Hammon has been extremely persistent, and insensitive to the class-
pride of the shoemakers, but he retires with some dignity and with some
claim on our sympathies.

LORD MAYOR

    Villain, thou told'st me that my daughter Rose
    This morning should be married at Saint Faith's:
    We have watched there these three hours at the least,   110
    Yet see we no such thing.

FIRK

    Truly, I am sorry for't: a bride's a pretty thing!

HODGE

    Come to the purpose: yonder's the bride and bridegroom
    you look for, I hope. Though you be lords, you are not to
    bar by your authority men from women, are you?   115

LORD MAYOR

    See, see, my daughter's masked!

LINCOLN   True, and my nephew,

    To hide his guilt, counterfeits him lame.

FIRK

    Yea, truly, God help the poor couple! They are lame and
    blind.

LORD MAYOR

    I'll ease her blindness.

LINCOLN   I'll his lameness cure.   120

FIRK

    [*Aside*] Lie down, sirs, and laugh! My fellow Ralph is
    taken for Rowland Lacy, and Jane for Mistress Damask
    Rose! This is all my knavery.

LORD MAYOR

    What, have I found you, minion?

LINCOLN   O base wretch!

    Nay, hide thy face, the horror of thy guilt   125
    Can hardly be washed off! Where are thy powers?
    What battles have you made? O yes, I see!
    Thou fought'st with Shame, and Shame hath conquered
        thee.
    This lameness will not serve.

LORD MAYOR   Unmask yourself.

LINCOLN

    Lead home your daughter.

LORD MAYOR   Take your nephew hence.   130

RALPH

    Hence? 'Swounds, what mean you? Are you mad? I hope

you cannot enforce my wife from me. Where's Hammon?

LORD MAYOR

Your wife?

LINCOLN

What Hammon?

RALPH

Yea, my wife: and therefore the proudest of you that lays   135
hands on her first, I'll lay my crutch cross his pate!

FIRK

To him, lame Ralph! Here's brave sport!

RALPH

Rose call you her? Why, her name is Jane! Look here else!
[*Unmasks* JANE] Do you know her now?

LINCOLN

Is this your daughter?

LORD MAYOR   No, nor this your nephew.   140
My Lord of Lincoln, we are both abused
By this base crafty varlet.

FIRK

Yea, forsooth no varlet, forsooth no base, forsooth I am
but mean; no crafty neither, but of the Gentle Craft.

LORD MAYOR

Where is my daughter Rose? Where is my child?   145

LINCOLN

Where is my nephew Lacy married?

FIRK

Why, here is good laced mutton, as I promised you.

LINCOLN

Villain, I'll have thee punished for this wrong!

FIRK

Punish the journeyman villain, but not the journeyman
shoemaker.   150

Enter DODGER

DODGER

My Lord, I come to bring unwelcome news:
Your nephew Lacy, and your daughter Rose
Early this morning wedded at the Savoy,
None being present but the Lady Mayoress.

147 *laced mutton* whore's flesh (with a pun on Lacy)

Besides, I learned among the officers,   155
The Lord Mayor vows to stand in their defence,
'Gainst any that shall seek to cross the match.

LINCOLN

Dares Eyre the shoemaker uphold the deed?

FIRK

Yes, sir: shoemakers dare stand in a woman's quarrel, I
warrant you, as deep as another, and deeper too.   160

DODGER

Besides, His Grace today dines with the Mayor,
Who on his knees humbly intends to fall,
And beg a pardon for your nephew's fault.

LINCOLN

But I'll prevent him. Come, Sir Roger Otley:
The King will do us justice in this cause.   165
Howe'er their hands have made them man and wife,
I will disjoin the match, or lose my life.

                  Exeunt [LINCOLN *and* LORD MAYOR]

FIRK

Adieu, Monsieur Dodger! Farewell, fools! Ha, ha! O if
they had stayed I would have so lammed them with flouts!
O heart! My codpiece-point is ready to fly in pieces every   170
time I think upon Mistress Rose, but let that pass, as my
Lady Mayoress says.

HODGE

This matter is answered. Come, Ralph, home with thy
wife! Come, my fine shoemakers, let's to our master's the
new Lord Mayor, and there swagger this Shrove Tuesday.   175
I'll promise you wine enough, for Madge keeps the cellar.

ALL

O rare! Madge is a good wench.

FIRK

And I'll promise you meat enough, for simpering Susan
keeps the larder. I'll lead you to victuals, my brave soldiers:
follow your captain! O brave! Hark, hark!   180

                Bell rings

159 *stand in a woman's quarrel.* Firk intends another bawdy *double-entendre.*
169 *lammed them with flouts* bombarded them with gibes
175 *swagger* make merry

ALL

The pancake bell rings! The pancake bell, trilill, my hearts!

FIRK

O brave! O sweet bell! O delicate pancakes! Open the doors, my hearts, and shut up the windows! Keep in the house, let out the pancakes! O rare, my hearts! Let's march together for the honour of Saint Hugh to the great new   185
hall in Gracious Street corner, which our master the new Lord Mayor hath built.

RALPH

O the crew of good fellows that will dine at my Lord Mayor's cost today!

HODGE

By the Lord, my Lord Mayor is a most brave man! How   190
shall prentices be bound to pray for him and the honour of the gentlemen shoemakers! Let's feed and be fat with my Lord's bounty.

FIRK

O musical bell still! O Hodge, O my brethren! There's cheer for the heavens! Venison pasties walk up and down,   195
piping hot, like sergeants; beef and brewis comes marching in dry fats; fritters and pancakes comes trowling in in wheelbarrows; hens and oranges hopping in porters' baskets; collops and eggs in scuttles; and tarts and custards comes quavering in in malt-shovels!   200

Enter more Prentices

ALL

Whoop! Look here, look here!

HODGE

How now, mad lads, whither away so fast?

1 PRENTICE

Whither? Why, to the great new hall! Know you not why? The Lord Mayor hath bidden all the prentices in London to breakfast this morning.   205

181 *The pancake bell* see note on V. i, 50
195 *pasties* ed. (pastimes Q1)
196 *brewis* thick broth
197 *fats* vats
197 *trowling* rolling
199 *collops* bacon   199 *scuttles* dishes

ALL

O brave shoemaker! O brave lord of incomprehensible
good fellowship! Whoo! Hark you, the pancake bell rings!

Cast up caps

FIRK

Nay, more, my hearts! Every Shrove Tuesday is our year
of jubilee, and when the pancake bell rings, we are as free
as my Lord Mayor. We may shut up our shops, and make   210
holiday. I'll have it called Saint Hugh's Holiday.

ALL

Agreed, agreed! Saint Hugh's Holiday!

HODGE

And this shall continue for ever.

ALL

O brave! Come, come, my hearts, away, away!

FIRK

O eternal credit to us of the Gentle Craft! March fair, my   215
hearts! O rare!

Exeunt

[Act V, Scene iii]

Enter KING *and his train over the stage*

KING

Is our Lord Mayor of London such a gallant?

NOBLEMAN

One of the merriest madcaps in your land.
Your Grace will think, when you behold the man,
He's rather a wild ruffian than a Mayor.
Yet thus much I'll ensure your Majesty: 5
In all his actions that concern his state,
He is as serious, provident, and wise,
As full of gravity amongst the grave,
As any Mayor hath been these many years.

KING

I am with child till I behold this huff-cap,   10

7 *provident* prudent
10 *with child* impatiently expecting   10 *huff-cap* madcap

But all my doubt is, when we come in presence,
His madness will be dashed clean out of countenance.

NOBLEMAN

It may be so, my Liege.

KING   Which to prevent,
Let someone give him notice 'tis our pleasure
That he put on his wonted merriment.   15
Set forward.

ALL

On afore.

Exeunt

[Act V, Scene iv]

Enter EYRE, HODGE, FIRK, RALPH, *and other Shoemakers,*
all with napkins on their shoulders

EYRE

Come, my fine Hodge, my jolly gentlemen shoemakers.
Soft, where be these cannibals, these varlets my officers?
Let them all walk and wait upon my brethren, for my
meaning is that none but shoemakers, none but the livery
of my Company shall in their satin hoods wait upon the   5
trencher of my Sovereign.

FIRK

O my Lord, it will be rare!

EYRE

No more, Firk! Come, lively! Let your fellow prentices
want no cheer; let wine be plentiful as beer, and beer as
water! Hang these penny-pinching fathers, that cram   10
wealth in innocent lambskins! Rip, knaves, avaunt, look to
my guests!

HODGE

My Lord, we are at our wits' end for room; those hundred
tables will not feast the fourth part of them!

11 *doubt* fear
15 *wonted* customary
 6 *trencher* dinner-plate
11 *innocent lambskins* i.e., purses

EYRE

Then cover me those hundred tables again, and again, till   15
all my jolly prentices be feasted. Avoid, Hodge; run,
Ralph; frisk about, my nimble Firk! Carouse me fathom
healths to the honour of the shoemakers! Do they drink
lively, Hodge? Do they tickle it, Firk?

FIRK

Tickle it? Some of them have taken their liquor standing so   20
long, that they can stand no longer. But for meat, they
would eat it, and they had it.

EYRE

Want they meat? Where's this swag-belly, this greasy
kitchen-stuff cook? Call the varlet to me! Want meat! Firk,
Hodge, lame Ralph, run, my tall men, beleaguer the   25
shambles, beggar all Eastcheap, serve me whole oxen in
chargers, and let sheep whine upon the tables like pigs for
want of good fellows to eat them! Want meat! Vanish,
Firk! Avaunt, Hodge!

HODGE

Your Lordship mistakes my man Firk: he means their   30
bellies want meat, not the boards, for they have drunk so
much they can eat nothing.

Enter LACY, ROSE, *and* MARGERY

MARGERY

Where is my Lord?

EYRE

How now, Lady Madgy?

MARGERY

The King's most excellent Majesty is new come! He sends   35
me for thy Honour: one of his most worshipful peers bade
me tell thou must be merry, and so forth, but let that pass.

EYRE

Is my Sovereign come? Vanish, my tall shoemakers, my
nimble brethren, look to my guests the prentices. Yet stay
a little: how now, Hans? How looks my little Rose?   40

19 *tickle it* set to with gusto (cf. III. iii, 72 and IV. ii, 7)
25 *beleaguer the shambles* besiege the meat-market
27 *chargers* large serving-dishes

LACY

Let me request you to remember me:
I know your Honour easily may obtain
Free pardon of the King for me and Rose,
And reconcile me to my uncle's grace.

EYRE

Have done, my good Hans, my honest journeyman. Look   45
cheerily: I'll fall upon both my knees till they be as hard
as horn, but I'll get thy pardon.

MARGERY

Good my Lord, have a care what you speak to his Grace.

EYRE

Away, you Islington whitepot! Hence, you hopperarse,
you barley pudding full of maggots, you broiled carbonado!   50
Avaunt, avaunt, Mephostophilus! Shall Sim Eyre learn to
speak of you, Lady Madgy? Vanish, Mother Miniver-cap,
vanish, go, trip and go, meddle with your partlets and your
pishery-pashery, your flewes and your whirligigs! Go, rub
out of mine alley! Sim Eyre knows how to speak to a Pope,   55
to Sultan Soliman, to Tamburlaine, and he were here: and
shall I melt, shall I droop before my Sovereign? No! Come,
my Lady Madgy; follow me, Hans; about your business, my
frolic free-booters; Firk, frisk about and about and about,
for the honour of mad Simon Eyre, Lord Mayor of London.   60

FIRK

Hey, for the honour of the shoemakers!

Exeunt

44 *grace* favour
49 *whitepot . . . hopperarse* rude allusions to the barrel-shape of Margery in
   her farthingale
50 *carbonado* steak
51 *learn* ed. (leaue Q1)
52 *Miniver-cap* headpiece trimmed with ermine
53 *partlets* linen collar with a small ruff
54 *flewes* the flaps of the French hood
54 *whirligigs* fripperies
54 *rub* be off

[Act V, Scene v]

A long flourish or two. Enter KING, *Nobles,* EYRE, MARGERY,
LACY, ROSE. LACY *and* ROSE *kneel*

KING

Well, Lacy, though the fact was very foul
Of your revolting from our kingly love
And your own duty, yet we pardon you.
Rise both, and, Mistress Lacy, thank my Lord Mayor
For your young bridegroom here.   5

EYRE

So, my dear Liege, Sim Eyre and my brethren the gentlemen shoemakers shall set your sweet Majesty's image cheek
by jowl by Saint Hugh, for this honour you have done
poor Simon Eyre. I beseech your Grace, pardon my rude
behaviour; I am a handicraftsman, yet my heart is without   10
craft. I would be sorry at my soul that my boldness should
offend my King.

KING

Nay, I pray thee, good Lord Mayor, be even as merry
As if thou wert among thy shoemakers:
It does me good to see thee in this humour.   15

EYRE

Sayest thou me so, my sweet Diocletian? Then hump!
Prince am I none, yet am I princely born. By the Lord of
Ludgate, I'll be as merry as a pie!

KING

Tell me in faith, mad Eyre, how old thou art.

EYRE

My Liege, a very boy, a stripling, a younker: you see not   20
a white hair on my head, not a grey in this beard. Every
hair, I assure thy Majesty, that sticks in this beard Sim
Eyre values at the King of Babylon's ransom; Tamar

1 *fact* deed
18 *pie* magpie
20 *younker* youth
23 *Tamar* ed. (Tama Q1) another name for Tamburlaine

16 *Diocletian.* A Roman emperor, here simply a term for 'majesty'.
16 *Then hump!* A catch-phrase of Eyre's: cf. 'cry hump' (27).

Cham's beard was a rubbing-brush to't: yet I'll shave it off
and stuff tennis balls with it, to please my bully King.   25

KING

But all this while I do not know your age.

EYRE

My Liege, I am six and fifty year old, yet I can cry hump
with a sound heart, for the honour of Saint Hugh. Mark
this old wench, my King: I danced the shaking of the
sheets with her six and thirty years ago, and yet I hope to   30
get two or three young Lord Mayors ere I die! I am lusty
still, Sim Eyre still: care and cold lodging brings white
hairs. My sweet Majesty, let care vanish, cast it upon thy
nobles; it will make thee look always young like Apollo, and
cry hump! Prince am I none, yet am I princely born.   35

KING

Ha, ha!
Say, Cornwall, didst thou ever see his like?

NOBLEMAN

Not I, my Lord.

Enter LINCOLN *and* LORD MAYOR

KING   Lincoln, what news with you?

LINCOLN

My gracious Lord, have care unto yourself,
For there are traitors here.

ALL   Traitors? Where? Who?   40

EYRE

Traitors in my house? God forbid! Where be my officers?
I'll spend my soul ere my King feel harm.

KING

Where is the traitor, Lincoln?

LINCOLN   Here he stands.

KING

Cornwall, lay hold on Lacy! Lincoln, speak:
What canst thou lay unto thy nephew's charge?   45

LINCOLN

This, my dear Liege: your Grace, to do me honour,
Heaped on the head of this degenerous boy

29 *shaking of the sheets* see note on IV. v, 82
47 *degenerous* degenerate

Desertless favours; you made choice of him,
To be commander over powers in France,
But he—

KING   Good Lincoln, prithee pause a while: 50
Even in thine eyes I read what thou wouldst speak.
I know how Lacy did neglect our love,
Ran himself deeply, in the highest degree,
Into vile treason.

LINCOLN   Is he not a traitor?

KING
Lincoln, he was; now have we pardoned him.   55
'Twas not a base want of true valour's fire
That held him out of France, but love's desire.

LINCOLN
I will not bear his shame upon my back.

KING
Nor shalt thou, Lincoln: I forgive you both.

LINCOLN
Then good my Leige, forbid the boy to wed   60
One whose mean birth will much disgrace his bed.

KING
Are they not married?

LINCOLN   No, my Liege.

BOTH   We are!

KING
Shall I divorce them then? O be it far
That any hand on earth should dare untie
The sacred knot knit by God's majesty!   65
I would not for my crown disjoin their hands
That are conjoined in holy nuptial bands.
How sayest thou, Lacy? Wouldst thou lose they Rose?

LACY
Not for all India's wealth, my Sovereign.

KING
But Rose, I am sure, her Lacy would forgo.   70

ROSE
If Rose were asked that question, she'd say no.

KING
You hear them, Lincoln?

69 *India's* ed. (Indians Q1)

LINCOLN   Yea, my Liege, I do.

KING

  Yet canst thou find i'th'heart to part these two?

  Who seeks, besides you, to divorce these lovers?

LORD MAYOR

  I do, my gracious Lord: I am her father.   75

KING

  Sir Roger Otley, our last Mayor, I think?

NOBLEMAN

  The same, my Liege.

KING   Would you offend Love's laws?

  Well, you shall have your wills; you sue to me

  To prohibit the match: soft, let me see:

  You both are married, Lacy, art thou not?   80

LACY

  I am, dread Sovereign.

KING   Then, upon thy life,

  I charge thee not to call this woman wife.

LORD MAYOR

  I thank your Grace.

ROSE   O my most gracious Lord! *Kneel*

KING

  Nay, Rose, never woo me; I'll tell you true,

  Although as yet I am a bachelor,   85

  Yet I believe I shall not marry you.

ROSE

  Can you divide the body from the soul,

  Yet make the body live?

KING   Yea, so profound?

  I cannot, Rose; but you I must divide:

  Fair maid, this bridegroom cannot be your bride.   90

  Are you pleased, Lincoln? Otley, are you pleased?

BOTH

  Yes, my Lord.

KING   Then must my heart be eased,

  For, credit me, my conscience lives in pain,

---

90 *this bridegroom cannot be your bride.* As Bowers points out, 'bride' could
  be used of either sex.

Till these whom I divorced be joined again.
Lacy, give me thy hand; Rose, lend me thine: 95
Be what you would be; kiss now; so, that's fine!
At night, lovers, to bed! Now, let me see,
Which of you all mislikes this harmony?

LORD MAYOR
Will you then take from me my child perforce?

KING
Why, tell me, Otley, shines not Lacy's name   100
As bright in the world's eyes as the gay beams
Of any citizen?

LINCOLN   Yea, but, my gracious Lord,
I do mislike the match far more than he:
Her blood is too too base.

KING   Lincoln, no more!
Dost thou not know that love repects no blood,   105
Cares not for difference of birth or state?
The maid is young, well born, fair, virtuous:
A worthy bride for any gentleman!
Beside, your nephew for her sake did stoop
To bare necessity, and, as I hear,   110
Forgetting honours and all courtly pleasures,
To gain her love became a shoemaker.
As for the honour which he lost in France,
Thus I redeem it: Lacy, kneel thee down!
Arise, Sir Rowland Lacy! Tell me now,   115
Tell me in earnest, Otley, canst thou chide,
Seeing thy Rose a lady and a bride?

LORD MAYOR
I am content with what your Grace hath done.

LINCOLN
And I, my Liege, since there's no remedy.

KING
Come on, then, all shake hands: I'll have you friends. 120
Where there is much love, all discord ends.
What says my mad Lord Mayor to all this love?

EYRE
O my Liege, this honour you have done to my fine journeyman here, Rowland Lacy, and all those favours which you
have shown to me this day in my poor house, will make   125

Simon Eyre live longer by one dozen of warm summers
more than he should.

KING

Nay, my mad Lord Mayor—that shall be thy name—
If any grace of mine can length thy life,
One honour more I'll do thee: that new building,   130
Which at thy cost in Cornhill is erected,
Shall take a name from us. We'll have it called
The Leadenhall, because in digging it
You found the lead that covereth the same.

EYRE

I thank your Majesty.   135

MARGERY

God bless your Grace.

KING

Lincoln, a word with you.

Enter HODGE, FIRK, RALPH, *and more Shoemakers*

EYRE

How now, my mad knaves? Peace, speak softly: yonder is
the King.

KING

With the old troop which there we keep in pay,   140
We will incorporate a new supply.
Before one summer more pass o'er my head,
France shall repent England was injured.
What are all those?

LACY   All shoemakers, my Liege,
Sometimes my fellows; in their companies   145
I lived as merry as an emperor.

KING

My mad Lord Mayor, are all these shoemakers?

EYRE

All shoemakers, my Liege, all gentlemen of the Gentle
Craft, true Trojans, courageous cordwainers; they all kneel
to the shrine of holy Saint Hugh.   150

---

130 *that new building*. See Introduction, p. **xi**.

ALL

God save your Majesty! All shoemakers!

KING

Mad Simon, would they anything with us?

EYRE

Mum, mad knaves, not a word! I'll do't, I warrant you.
They are all beggars, my Liege, all for themselves; and I
for them all on both my knees do entreat that for the   155
honour of poor Simon Eyre, and the good of his brethren
these mad knaves, your Grace would vouchsafe some
privilege to my new Leadenhall, that it may be lawful for
us to buy and sell leather there two days a week.

KING

Mad Sim, I grant your suit: you shall have patent   160
To hold two market days in Leadenhall;
Mondays and Fridays, those shall be the times.
Will this content you?

ALL

Jesus bless your Grace!

EYRE

In the name of these my poor brethren shoemakers, I most   165
humbly thank your Grace. But before I rise, seeing you are
in the giving vein, and we in the begging, grant Sim Eyre
one boon more.

KING

What is it, my Lord Mayor?

EYRE

Vouchsafe to taste of a poor banquet that stands sweetly   170
waiting for your sweet presence.

KING

I shall undo thee Eyre, only with feasts.
Already have I been too troublesome:
Say, have I not?

EYRE

O my dear King, Sim Eyre was taken unawares upon a day   175
of shroving which I promised long ago to the prentices of
London, for, and't please your Highness, in time past,

---

151 *All shoemakers* ed. (all shoomaker Q1). Some editors make this a stage
       direction
160 *patent* letters patent, royal licence

I bare the water-tankard, and my coat
Sits not a whit the worse upon my back.
And then, upon a morning, some mad boys   180
—It was Shrove Tuesday even as 'tis now—gave me my
breakfast, and I swore then by the stopple of my tankard,
if ever I came to be Lord Mayor of London, I would feast
all the prentices. This day, my Liege, I did it, and the
slaves had an hundred tables five times covered. They are   185
gone home and vanished:
Yet add more honour to the Gentle Trade:
Taste of Eyre's banquet, Simon's happy made.

KING

Eyre, I will taste of thy banquet, and will say,
I have not met more pleasure on a day.   190
Friends of the Gentle Craft, thanks to you all!
Thanks, my kind Lady Mayoress, for our cheer.
Come, Lords, a while let's revel it at home:
When all our sports and banquetings are done,
Wars must right wrongs which Frenchmen have begun.   195

Exeunt

FINIS

---

178 *I bare the water-tankard, and my coat.* The shift from prose to verse
     occurs at the beginning of K4 verso in Q1, although 'for, and't please
     your Highness, in time past', the final words on K4 recto, also form a
     line of blank verse.
187 *Yet add more honour* . . . This couplet is set as prose in Q1.